BERLIN AIRLIFT

BERLIN AIRLIFT

AIR BRIDGE TO FREEDOM

A PHOTOGRAPHIC HISTORY OF THE GREAT AIRLIFT

BRUCE McALLISTER

Roundup Press

P.O. Box 109

Boulder, CO 80306-0109

USA

www.wingsalcan.com

ISBN 978-0-615-98499-5

Library of Congress Control Number 2014911716

Book Design & Layout: Elizabeth Watson, Watson Graphics,

Photography Editor: Bruce McAllister

Printed by: C & C Offset Printing, China

DISCLAIMER

The author has attempted to be accurate in listing aeronautical information. He cannot be held responsible for the accuracy of this information.

DEDICATION

To the 73 Allied airmen

who made the ultimate sacrifice

during the Berlin Airlift

ACKNOWLEDGMENTS

Alliierten Museum Berlin- Bernd von Kostka

Bundesarchiv

National Museum of the United States Air Forces

Imperial War Museum, London

Landesarchiv Berlin- Barbara Schäche

Harry S. Truman Library & Museum

Gina McNeely-Photo Researcher

CONTENTS

INTRODUCTION

9

1. PRELUDE

17

2. OPERATION VITTLES

25

3. THE AIRLIFT PILOTS

61

4. UPGRADING THE AIRFIELDS

79

5. SUPPLYING THE WEST BERLINERS

103

6. THE CANDY BOMBER

129

7. THE AIRCRAFT

137

8. THE MAINTENANCE

159

9. THE AIR CRASHES

173

10. AFTERMATH

183

BIBLIOGRAPHY   216

INTRODUCTION

This photographic history of the Berlin Airlift will hopefully immerse the reader in what is remembered as the greatest airlift of all time. It pays tribute not only to the more than 70 Allied pilots who lost their lives flying through bad weather and with minimum rest, but also to the great people of Berlin who suffered through a blockade that choked off electricity, food, and coal. Nothing would break the spirit of the West Berliners. As President John F. Kennedy later said, in honor of the Berliners' resilience, "Ich bin ein Berliner." In a major television address in West Berlin on July 25, 1961, he described the embattled city as "the great testing place of Western courage and will" and declared that any attack on West Berlin would be viewed as an attack on the United States.

◄ Churchill, Truman, and Stalin meet before the Potsdam Conference in 1945. They were all smiles but there was little trust between the Allies and Stalin. NARA

(Overleaf spread)
► On June 13, 1945, Marshal Bernard Montgomery (head not showing), General of the Army, Dwight Eisenhower, and General Georgi Zhukov toasted each other, celebrating the end of World War II. Later, Zhukov was not so accommodating – he told the Allies that the Soviet Union considered their access to Berlin as a privilege, not as a right. NARA

►► From July 17 to August 2, 1945, in Berlin, the Potsdam Conference dealt with questions about the future of Germany. Stalin is on the right and Churchill is seated above the flags. Truman is lower left with both of his hands on the table. NARA

◄ ◄ Although the Marshall Plan did not help Berlin before the Airlift, it did help rebuild West Germany and much of Europe. It was a thorn in the side of the Russians and they greeted it with silence.
© Bundesarchiv

◄ Lt. General Lucius Clay greeted General of the Army, Dwight D. Eisenhower, upon his arrival in Berlin in 1945. Eisenhower was there to attend the Potsdam Conference.
Library of Congress

► Truman used the B-29 Superfortress as a diplomatic weapon in the Cold War. He sent several to Europe during the Berlin Airlift, knowing the Russians thought they had nuclear weapons on board. They did not.
USAF

◄ Wilhelm Pieck, Communist Party leader of East Germany (Left), with Stalin, attends a memorial service in East Berlin. The two leaders engineered the Berlin Blockade. Date unknown.

© BUNDESARCHIV

► In the late 1940s a huge portrait of Joseph Stalin dominated the SED Central Committee headquarters in East Berlin.

© BUNDESARCHIV

STUDIERT STALIN
LERNT VON STALIN
STALIN
Stalin der beste Freund
Volkes!
J·W·STALIN
Der Führer und Lehrer der Menschheit im Kampf
für Frieden, Demokratie und Sozialismus
Vorwärts, unter d

◄◄ In 1948, when the city of West Berlin was *first* isolated from West Germany, and the Airlift started, things were looking normal in this view from the Funkturm Tower, except for lack of traffic on the autobahn. The famous Avus racetrack is in the center of the photograph.
AUTHOR'S COLLECTION

◄ In April 1948, all of the military trains were stored at the Grunewald Bahnhof when the Allies refused newly imposed Russian regulations and inspections *as they* made their runs to West Germany. Consequently, the Allies resorted to the Berlin Airlift as a way to circumnavigate the Russian tactics.
NARA

1. PRELUDE

From the end of World War II Soviet Premier Joseph Stalin had but one goal in mind and that was to force the Allies out of Berlin, and hence all of Germany, thus consolidating Russia's gains in East Europe. Czechoslovakia had already fallen prey to the Communists.

Berlin was the choke point. After World War II the Russians had stripped Berlin of anything that moved or which they could get their hands on. The population of Berlin had been cut in half—from four million to a little more than two million, and the male population consisted mostly of boys and old men. Downtown Berlin had been turned into a smoking ruin. Gas, electricity, telephone service, and water were no longer available. Most of the city's bridges had been destroyed and transportation around Berlin was non-existent.

While women were always victims of sexual violence during wartime, in May 1945, "Reparations succeeded rape as the Communist Order of the Day. Records show over 100,000 women were raped in Berlin, and that 90 percent of the city's women contracted venereal diseases. Ninety percent of Berlin's steel industry, 75 percent of its printing industry, 85 percent of the machinery of the electrical and optical industries were loaded onto flatcars for shipment to the Soviet Union."[1] The Russians were going to fight the Allies tooth and nail and were determined to control all of what was left of Berlin.

Initially, before the Allies had moved into their sectors of Berlin, the Russians set up a puppet government, controlled the utilities, and even the press. By 1948, any hope for cooperation of the Soviets in the joint government of Germany had all but failed. And Stalin, in a note to Wilhelm Pieck, Communist Party leader of East Germany, had remarked, "Let's make a joint effort, perhaps we can kick them out."[2]

A game of cat-and-mouse ensued. The Russians periodically held up trains, vehicles and barges linking West Germany to West Berlin. But the Russians had overlooked something very important: Air corridors.

Russian General Georgi Zhukov and U.S. General Lucius Clay had verbally agreed, "all traffic–air, road and rail…would be free from border search or control by customs or military authorities."[3] Both had overlooked the importance of air corridors. At the time of this loose agreement, Clay did not realize that the Soviets would use border and customs control as an excuse to start the blockade of Berlin. Luckily, the Russians did not figure out how to block the three air corridors the Allies ended up using to continue supplying the Occupation Forces and West Berlin's population.

For the Allies, setting up some sort of government in Berlin became a nightmare. "The Commission decided that the city must be the seat of the Allied Control Council and that it would have to be administered as one unit by the Kommandatura of the three Military Commandants.

EAST GERMAN POLICE BARRIER
(SURRENDER PASS)

EAST GERMAN CUSTOMS POLICE BARRIER
(NO PASS SURRENDER)

SOVIET CHECKPOINT

EAST GERMAN BARRIER
(SOVIET SOLDIER MEETS YOU HERE)

WEST GERMAN BARRIER

ALPHA CHECKPOINT

WEST GERMAN BARRIER

◀ ◀ The Helmstedt checkpoint during the Cold War. Date unknown. AUTHOR'S COLLECTION

◀ This U.S. Air Force aerial photograph was taken during the Soviet "Little Blockade" on the autobahn between Berlin and Helmstedt, West Germany. Only four trucks per hour were allowed through the checkpoint at Helmstedt. NARA

Yet as in the ACC, all Kommandatura decisions must be unanimous. Each Commandant had a veto. Deadlock had been built into the system–and, in due course, would wreck it."[4] It did not take long for things to degrade in the Kommandatura. At a key meeting, Russian Colonel Yelizarov stood and took offense at U.S. Army Colonel Frank Howley's departure (he had been excused by the chair

of the Kommandatura and surprised the Allies with the blockade.

Other things contributed to the breakup. There was a push for currency reform in West Germany, followed by one in both West Berlin and East Berlin. Ultimately, West Berlin and East Berlin planned for separate currencies that were interchangeable at par. But this gave the Soviets a pretext to intimidate the city government and they sent in thugs to block approval of the currencies. When things calmed down, the city assembly agreed that the Soviet backed currency would apply only to East Berlin and not West Berlin. West Berliners were nervous about the rival currency measures. "Should they convert some of their money to *Ostmarks* as a precaution against Allied withdrawal?"[6]

But unbeknownst to the Allies, the Soviets had planned to blockade Berlin within days. "In the end, the breakup of the Allied Kommandatura had been a planned work in progress for quite some time, according to Howley, as it suited the purposes of the Soviets, period. It followed the pattern of the breakup of the Allied Control Council, when three months earlier Marshal Sokolovsky staged the walkout then."[7]

of the meeting), "and labeled it a "hooligan action." Howley and Yelizarov already had a contentious history. Howley described him as a "big, powerful, bruiser," who hunted wild boar with a machine gun in the woods outside Berlin, and once said, "He and I always kept one hand on the trigger."[5] It was only a matter of time before the Russians walked out

ENDNOTES

1 Jean E. Smith, *The Defense of Berlin*, p.67
2 Richard Reeves, *Daring Young Men*, p. xv
3 Lucius Clay, *Decision in Germany*, p. 26
4 A. & J. Tusa, *The Berlin Airlift*, p. 12
5 Brig. General Frank Howley, *Berlin Command*, pages 180-181
6 Jean E. Smith, *The Defense of Berlin*, p.116
7 Ibid

◄◄ At his first Kommandantura meeting, Colonel Frank Howley held his own with the uncooperative Russian delegation, discussing the administration of Berlin. Front to rear, left side of table are: General E. O. Herbert representing the British, Colonel Frank L. Howley representing the United States. Front to rear right side of table: General Jean Ganeval representing the French; General Kotikov representing the Russians; and Colonel Yalizarov, deputy to the Russian Commandant. NARA

◄ General Frank "Howlin" Howley after the Airlift ended. He served over four years as Military Governor in West Berlin, first as deputy, and then as Commandant of the U.S. Sector. He forbid U.S. forces from fraternizing with Russians while we were losing Airlift pilots. AUTHOR'S COLLECTION

▲ An aerial photo of Tempelhof Airfield in 1945. Precision bombing in World War II left Tempelhof's buildings intact and the main runway and taxiways in reasonable shape. Eleven C-47s are visible in this photograph. USAREUR

▶ (1-1B) Kaiser Wilhelm Memorial Church barely survived World War II but was a symbol of West Berlin's rebirth. In a bombing raid in 1943, the church was largely destroyed but part of the spire and much of the entrance hall survived. This photo was taken before the Airlift began. AUTHOR'S COLLECTION

2. OPERATION VITTLES

As the greatest airlift in history, "Operation Vittles" (or as the British named their

effort "Operation Plainfare") was a masterpiece in coordination between the Allies.

From coordinating the use of many different types of aircraft with different airspeeds,

► In 1948, Douglas C-47s
unloading at Tempelhof Airport
in West Berlin.
USAF NATIONAL MUSEUM

to fighting winter weather, and putting up with Russian interference in the form of anti-aircraft fire, searchlights, and Yak-3 fighter buzzing, the Allies were fighting an uphill battle.

The United States drew on its worldwide inventory of C-54 Skymaster aircraft. The C-54 could carry more cargo efficiently than any other aircraft, and making the Skymaster the workhorse for the Airlift simplified maintenance – mechanics could concentrate more on the C-54 aircraft and its replacement parts and engines. The Air Force gathered and ferried C-54s from around the world while early on,

C-47s and RAF Dakotas did an admirable job getting critical supplies into West Berlin.

After President Harry Truman committed the United States to the Berlin Airlift by furnishing 75 C-54s, General Curtis LeMay was charged with organizing and coordinating it. He brought in General William H. Tunner, who had coordinated the "Hump" Airlift over the Himalaya Mountains from India to China during World War II.

Tunner was well suited to the job and had the experience to turn what was a "cowboy" operation into a well coordinated, tightly run airlift.

Although over 540 Allied military aircraft participated in the Airlift, that number did not include civilian aircraft chartered from non-scheduled airlines. Yet, "No plane was immune. A British Dakota took off for Berlin with the loading crew still on board in the back. An American

▼ C-54s unload their cargo during the round-the-clock operation of the Berlin Airlift. USAF NATIONAL MUSEUM

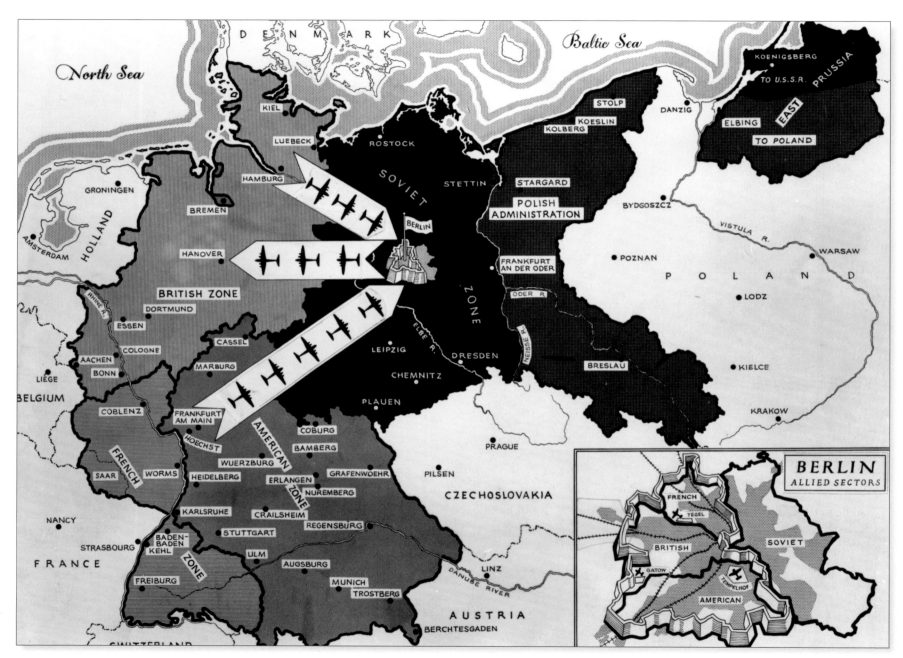

North Sea

DENMARK

Baltic Sea

KIEL

LUEBECK

HAMBURG

GRONINGEN

BREMEN

ROSTOCK

STETTIN

KOENIGSBERG

TO U.S.S.R.

EAST PRUSSIA

ELBING

TO POLAND

STOLP

KOESLIN

KOLBERG

DANZIG

SOVIET

BERLIN

POLISH
ADMINISTRATION

STARGARD

BYDGOSZCZ

VISTULA R.

HOLLAND

AMSTERDAM

HANOVER

BRITISH ZONE

DORTMUND

ESSEN

RHINE R.

COLOGNE

AACHEN

BONN

LIÉGE

BELGIUM

COBLENZ

FRANKFURT
AM MAIN

HOECHST

FRENCH

SAAR

WORMS

CASSEL

MARBURG

LEIPZIG

CHEMNITZ

PLAUEN

ZONE

FRANKFURT
AN DER ODER

ODER R.

NEISSE R.

ELBE R.

DRESDEN

BRESLAU

POZNAN

WARSAW

POLAND

LODZ

KIELCE

KRAKOW

AMERICAN

ZONE

COBURG

BAMBERG

WUERZBURG

ERLANGEN

NUREMBERG

GRAFENWOEHR

PRAGUE

PILSEN

CZECHOSLOVAKIA

HEIDELBERG

KARLSRUHE

CRAILSHEIM

REGENSBURG

NANCY

BADEN-
BADEN

KEHL

STRASBOURG

FRANCE

FREIBURG

ZONE

STUTTGART

ULM

AUGSBURG

MUNICH

TROSTBERG

LINZ

DANUBE RIVER

AUSTRIA

BERCHTESGADEN

SWITZERLAND

BERLIN
ALLIED SECTORS

FRENCH

TEGEL

BRITISH

GATOW

SOVIET

TEMPELHOF

AMERICAN

▲ This map shows the three corridors the Allies used to get vital spplies to Berlin during the Airlift. Author's Collection

diplomat high-ranking enough to have his own C-47 flew to Frankfurt for meetings, then came back to Rhein-Main and found that his plane had been stripped and loaded with three tons of flour. In London, the RAF requisitioned two C-47s from Ciro's, the fanciest nightclub in the city, which had been using the planes to ferry customers to the pleasures of the French Riviera."[1]

"The *New Yorker* estimated that over 70,000 people were involved, 45,000 German loaders and workers, 12,000 U.S.A.F. personnel, 8,000 R.A.F. personnel (including Australians, New Zealanders, and South Africans); 3,000 displaced persons from Baltic states, 800 U.S.

Naval, and 2,000 U.S. Army Airlift Support personnel."[2]

On August 13, 1948, Berlin had one of its worst storms in decades and by chance General Tunner was flying in to Tempelhof that day. Three U.S. Air Force aircraft had major problems (two crash-landed) and the controllers could not handle the backed-up traffic (see Chapter 8). Tunner recalled "Bob Hope once saying, "Soup I can take but this stuff has noodles in it."[3] Because of this memorable day's fiascos, General Tunner changed many procedures; there would be no stacking on inbound flights to Tempelhof. If an aircraft could not land on the first approach, it would immediately return to West Germany with its valuable cargo.

◀ General Lucius Clay (center) and fellow Allied officers look over a model layout of loading operations for the Berlin Airlift. AUTHOR'S COLLECTION

▲ On October 14, 1948, at the beginning of the Berlin Airlift, U. S. Army General Lucius Clay (second from left) and his British counterpart meet with German workers in West Berlin. NATIONAL ARCHIVES

▲ By mid-August of 1948, Lieutenant General William Tunner had added 72 C-54s to the effort and brought in two-thirds of all U.S. Air Force C-54 aircrews worldwide to fly the airlift 24 hours a day. Tunner brought such a level of organization to the Berlin operation that the per-day tonnage brought into West Berlin by the planes eventually exceeded the amount of material that had been brought in by train. Immediately upon arrival, he initiated a new "straight-in approach" technique that enabled 16 aircraft to be brought in over a period of one and one-half hours instead of the nine under the old system.

USAF NATIONAL MUSEUM

The British also worked on improving their operations. "The RAF sanction to get pilots to land the first time was to make them fill out a form if they overshot. It was a detested chore."[4]

In September, the Russians decided to test the Allied pilots by conducting mock aerial dogfights and totally ignoring air safety. They also practiced anti-aircraft firing–"one day so heavily that all the windows at Gatow were rattled by the shelling. There were mock attacks on allied planes, large scale maneuvers and aerial target practices in the corridors."[5]

"To demonstrate the Airlift's potential to the Soviets and the world, Tunner put on a spectacular show over the 24-hour period ending at noon, Easter Sunday, April 16, 1949, dubbed the "Easter Parade." During this period, 1,398 flights delivered almost 13,000 tons of coal to Berlin... The airbridge had, on a single day, handled the equivalent of 600

rail cars of coal without injury or accident."[6] In retrospect, "Operation Vittles" accomplished all of its objectives—it kept West Berlin alive and it stifled the Russians' attempts to push the Allies out of Berlin.

ENDNOTES
1 Richard Reeves, *Daring Young Men*, p. 39-40
2 J. Provan & R. Davies, *Berlin Airlift*, p. 78
3 A. & J. Tusa, *The Berlin Airlift*, p. 246
4 Ibid, p. 247
5 Ibid, p. 249
6 D. Giangreco and Robert Griffin, *Airbridge to Berlin*, p. 182

▲ (Center) General William Tunner.
USAF NATIONAL MUSEUM

▲ (Right) Lieutenant General Curtis E. LeMay shares dinner with a staff sergeant during the Berlin Airlift. LeMay was instrumental in making the airlift work efficiently.
NARA

◄ (Overleaf) In 1948, a C-54 aircraft landing at Tempelhof Airport during the Berlin Airlift. The Airlift supported the Allied troops and over two million civilians.
LIBRARY OF CONGRESS

▼ Early in the Berlin Airlift, C-47s unload their cargo at Tempelhof Airfield, West Berlin.
AUTHOR'S COLLECTION

THE WHITE HOUSE
WASHINGTON

To The Men and Women of the Berlin Airlift

This visit to Germany by Vice President elect Barkley affords me an ideal opportunity to express to you who are engaged in the Berlin airlift my deep appreciation of your outstanding service.

The Berlin Airlift, under the direction of our Air Force, is an achievement of historic and far-reaching significance, by the joint efforts of our Army, Navy, and Air Force, together with the forces of Great Britain and France. It expresses the unity of the Western nations in the cause of peace.

Operation Vittles has assured the world of our faith in our ideals. We are grateful to all of you who have made this possible.

At this Christmas Season the American people are thinking of you and your loved ones. On their behalf, I again wish you a very Merry Christmas.

December 21, 1948

Harry Truman

▲ A 1948 Christmas card to all personnel of the Berlin Airlift from President Harry S. Truman.
NARA

▶ Douglas Aircraft produced this ad, highlighting its contribution to the Berlin Airlift.
AUTHOR'S COLLECTION

"Operation Vittles"
YANKEE FLIERS IN DOUGLAS PLANES CARRY OUT GREATEST AIR ASSIGNMENT IN HISTORY

Crack pilots and the hard-working crews of the U.S. Air Force, using Douglas air transports exclusively, have flown over 150,000 tons of food, fuel, medicines and equipment into Berlin since June 26.

This has been the most impressive demonstration of transportation by air the world has ever seen. It has proved that a city of two million people can be kept supplied with the necessities of life by air transport alone.

All told—Douglas air transports have logged over 7,000,000 miles since the air lift began. 'Round the clock —in all kinds of weather—dependable Douglas planes have been flying in and out of Templehof Airport at the rate of one every two minutes. This is a record of which the Air Force and Douglas can be justly proud.

But remember this: these Douglas planes are of a design created by Douglas *prior to the last war!* They can be compared only in dependability to the larger, faster Douglas transports now being built.

"Operation Vittles" points squarely to the vital necessity of transport aircraft—both in times of peace and times of war. If America has to fight again, air power will again be decisive. To gain and hold the "air heads" of any future conflict, great fleets of modern air transports will prove strategic weapons of prime importance.

DOUGLAS AIRCRAFT COMPANY, INC., SANTA MONICA, CALIFORNIA

★
AIR TRANSPORT
—servant of peace
..weapon of defense
★
DOUGLAS

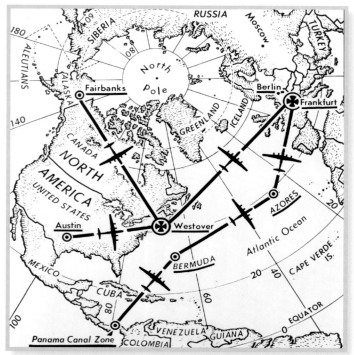

▲ Map showing routes of C-54 Skymasters from the United States to Frankfurt, Germany, in 1948 during the Berlin Airlift.
LIBRARY OF CONGRESS

▲ U.S. Navy R-5D aircraft came from as far away as the Pacific Theatre to support the Berlin Airlift. The first 24 R-5Ds to arrive in Germany were greeted with freezing rain at Rhein-Main Airport.
COURTESY NAVY HISTORICAL FOUNDATION

▶ Unloading a U.S. Navy R-5D during the Berlin Airlift.
COURTESY U. S. NAVY

▶ (Bottom) n October 1948, a passenger on a U. S. Air Force C-47 supply run photographed this Soviet YAK-3 fighter as it "buzzed" the C-47. The Russians often harassed Allied Airlift aircraft even though they were inside their approved air corridors.
AUTHOR'S COLLECTION

▶ At Bremerhaven, hundreds of miles from the nearest Airlift airfield, aviation fuel for Airlift aircraft flows ashore from a U. S. Navy tanker.
USAF NATIONAL MUSEUM

◄ At Rhein-Main Airfield, a C-54 Skymaster refueling during the Berlin Airlift.
USAF National Museum

▲ At Wiesbaden Air Force Base, power station equipment is loaded onto a U. S. Air Force Fairchild C-82 Packet aircraft for shipment to West Berlin. Date unknown.
USAF National Museum

▲ View from the control tower at Celle airfield in West Germany. A number of Douglas C-54 Skymaster aircraft are being loaded for flights to West Berlin. IMPERIAL WAR MUSEUM

▲ Allied personnel monitor Airlift flights with the help of radar. Date and location unknown.
USAF National Museum

▲ A U. S. Air Force sergeant monitors a GCA (Ground Controlled
Approach) approach into Tempelhof Airfield.
© Provan–AlliiertenMuseum / Berlin

▼ (Below and facing page) RAF control tower
personnel at work on the night shift at West Berlin .
© AlliiertenMuseum / Berlin

► A weather
officer at
Oberpfaffenhofen
Air Force Depot
briefs the crew of
a B-17 before its
six-hour patrol
of the corridors.
Every seventh
aircraft flying the
Airlift had a radio
operator who
reported weather
conditions in code
at four designated
points in each
corridor.
USAF

▶ In June 1948, at Tempelhof Airfield, a sergeant keeps flight arrival board up to date. It appears that most of the Airlift flights that day were running on time.
NARA

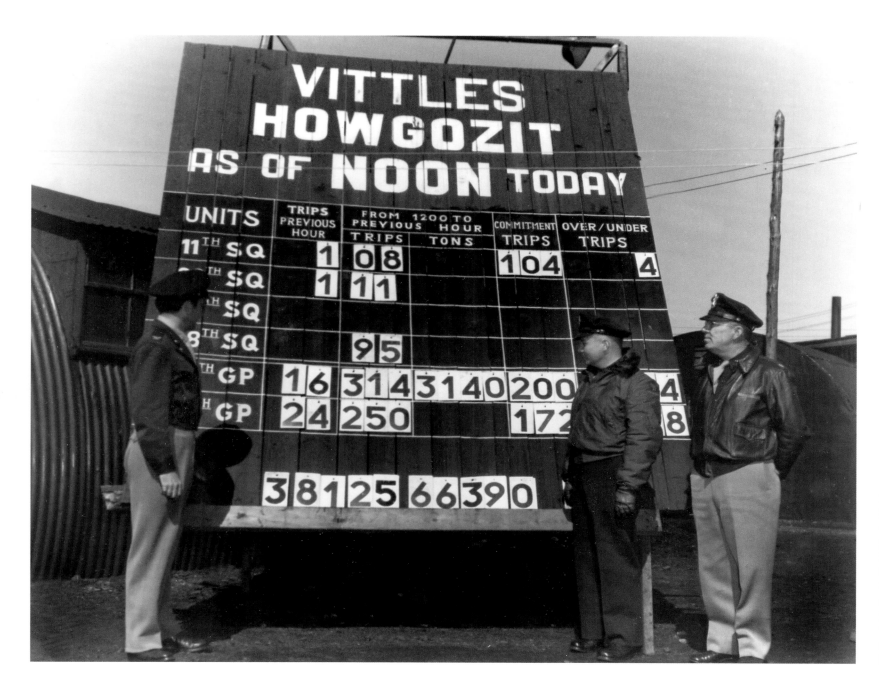

UNITS	TRIPS PREVIOUS HOUR	FROM 1200 TO PREVIOUS HOUR		COMMITMENT	OVER/UNDER
		TRIPS	TONS	TRIPS	TRIPS
11TH SQ	1	08		104	4
TH SQ	1	11			
TH SQ					
8TH SQ		95			
TH GP	16	314	3140	200	4
H GP	24	250		172	8

3 8 1 2 5 6 6 3 9 0

◄ This "HOWGOZIT" board kept Fassberg Airfield personnel up to date on the number of flights and tonnage flown to West Berlin. USAF NATIONAL MUSEUM

▲ In West Germany, a RAF Avro York taxis by 4 U.S. Air Force C-54s awaiting their cargo of vital supplies for West Berlin.

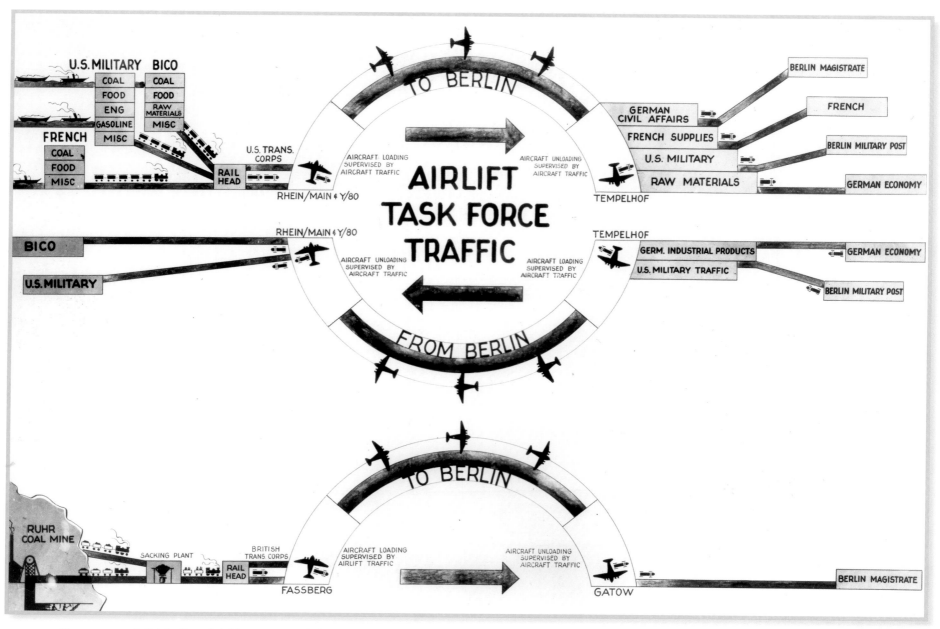

The source and distribution of airlift cargoes carried to and from Berlin by United States Air Force aircraft is shown in this chart. The flow of cargo carried by British planes is not included; only supplies carried by USAF planes operating at Rhein-Main and Wiesbaden Air Force Bases and from the Fassberg RAF Airfield.

► In Frankfurt during the Berlin Airlift, these German barges were used as floating warehouses for food that would be airlifted to West Berlin. Approximately 18,000 tons of food was stocked on the barges.

▲ Crews unload 25 tons of flour through the lower elevator of the giant Douglas C-74 Globemaster on one of its first trips to West Berlin.
USAF NATIONAL MUSEUM

▶ During the early stages of the Berlin Airlift, workers unload badly needed flour from a C-47 at Berlin's Tempelhof Airfield.
NARA

► At Rhein-Main Airfield, two men load milk for shipment to West Berlin.
USAF National Museum

► In 1948, barrels of machine oil being loaded into a C-47 aircraft for shipment from Rhein-Main to West Berlin.
Library of Congress

◀ Unloading coal from C-54s was labor intensive. USAF NATIONAL MUSEUM

▶ West German laborers load coal into bags for shipment to West Berlin. AUTHOR'S COLLECTION

◄ Duffle bags were often used to carry coal to West Berlin. USAF NATIONAL MUSEUM

► Coal fresh off Airlift aircraft is unloaded from trucks onto barges in West Berlin for distribution throughout the Allied Sectors. USAF NATIONAL MUSEUM

◄ Berlin Airlift flights continued around the clock —day and night, seven days a week. C-47s and C-54s flew food and other critical supplies into the western Sectors of Berlin.
NARA

► A British enlisted man directs the parking of a coal truck as German laborers prepare to load a shipment of coal aboard a U.S. Air Force C-54 at Fassberg Air Field before its flight to West Berlin.
USAF National Museum

◄ At Fassberg RAF Station in West Germany, Allied personnel secure coal in a U.S. Air Force C-54 in preparation for flight to West Berlin. One veteran, Lloyd Banquer, recalls "The C-47s I was radio operating in out of Rabat in '53 and '54 still had coal and potato dust from the Airlift." USAF NATIONAL MUSEUM

► Twenty German Youth Activities boys helped load light crates onto trucks at Tempelhof Airfield in West Berlin. NARA

◄◄ Two U. S. Navy pilots double-checked their course as they entered the Russian zone en route to West Berlin. The Navy contributed two squadrons of R-5D Skymasters to the Airlift. NARA

◄ U. S. Air Force Captain Baker (second from left) receives his flight plan in the 48th Troop Carrier Squadron operations room before taking off on a night flight. NARA

►► (Overleaf left) In September 1948, Captain Brady Cole checks his instrument approach plate as he nears West Berlin with the largest cargo ever carried during the Airlift. Instruments shown indicate that the C-74 Globemaster was cruising at over 230 miles per hour with a 25-ton load. NARA

3. THE AIRLIFT PILOTS

Early on in the Airlift, pilots, crews, loaders, and controllers received very little time off. Bad weather and corrosive coal dust, combined with the lack of organized aircraft maintenance schedules, made their jobs even more difficult and dangerous.

► Berlin Airlift pilots receive their final orders before flying another load of coal out of Rhein-Main Air Base in July, 1948. AUTHOR'S COLLECTION

U.S. Air Force pilots typically flew two round trips from various airfields in West Germany to Berlin every day, with each round trip taking between six and eight hours. As General Tunner fine-tuned schedules, ground time at Tempelhof was cut by using mobile snack bars. Young Berlin Red Cross women would drive the snack bars to the flight crews as they unloaded their valuable cargo, and offer them coffee and doughnuts.

"Lieutenant John Townsend of Lompoc, California, wrote home of airmen having terrific problems with dust in their eyes, some of them literally spending days in hospitals where doctors had to remove eyeballs from sockets to clean out coal dust."[1] "The USAF discovered that some of their men were on duty for seven days a week. If they were lucky they got seven hours' sleep in a thirty-two hour period. They kept awake by drinking coffee…Exhaustion was certainly taking

◄ (Far left) A C-54 crew coordinates during a critical phase of their flight into West Berlin.
USAF National Museum

▲ (Above middle) In 1949, a U.S. Air Force C-54 radio operator takes a catnap during an Airlift flight into Tempelhof Airfield.
Author's Collection

▲ Engineer Arthur J. Poole made 86 missions over "The Hump" and 30 bombing missions over Germany during World War II before landing a job on the Airlift.
NARA

◄ A U. S. Air Force Airlift pilot after a long day's work.
© AlliiertenMuseum / Berlin

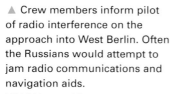

▲ Crew members inform pilot of radio interference on the approach into West Berlin. Often the Russians would attempt to jam radio communications and navigation aids.
USAF National Museum

its toll. Pilots routinely forgot to take their engines off boost, put down their flaps or feather their engines, and they were more irritable, as one pilot admitted: 'I also notice that when I am tired, people I normally dislike mildly I began to dislike very much indeed.'[2]

Other pilots spent even more time on continuous duty. Lieutenant Colonel Harold Watson, at the time of the Airlift, was recalled from his job as a TWA pilot. "At my base, Celle, we were assigned twelve hours of duty per day during which we made three flights per day regardless of the weather for ten days. Then we were given three says off before starting another ten day shift. You can imagine what a tight schedule we were on and we operated regardless of weather and our headings were all made with the help of ground control radar approach."[3]

Fog was a big problem in the winter for all pilots. One "night of impenetrable fog halted operations at Tempelhof and Gatow for ten hours; Allied pilots were getting 'cold feet,' claimed a writer in *Tägliche Rundschau*, because of the weather and inferior planes, but in late morning the two airports began receiving traffic again. 'We flew,' pilots like

"YEP, I FEEL RIGHT AT HOME SINCE THEY MODIFIED OUR C-54 COCKPITS!"

▲ A cartoon about the U.S. Navy pilots who participated in the Berlin Airlift.
AUTHOR'S COLLECTION

to say, when birds walked." On the thirtieth of November, General Tunner "reported, the city (Berlin) was smothered by a pea-souper so dense that 'you couldn't drive a car.' That day only one plane landed."[4]

Some pilots had wild experiences flying the Airlift. Major Bill Anderson, who was an Airlift pilot for nine months, recalled "We were making our last trip for the night, we were taking off from our base at Celle Royal Air Force station. The weather was pretty good, overcast with about 600-foot ceiling. I was cleared for take off. With full power we took off and started on course in the overcast. I asked the copilot to set our climb power. At that time our #2 engine did not respond. When I looked at #2 engine I saw oil spewing over the top of the engine. The hydraulic oil line that controls the prop pitch had broken and the engine had gone to full high RPM and was exceeding the engine limits. Despite all efforts to stop the engine it ran out of oil and the engine seized. The sudden stoppage caused the propeller shaft to sheer and the propeller flew off in to the side of the aircraft behind the cockpit area into the radio compartment, and knocked out all our radios. To make a long story short, I found a break in the clouds and let down under the overcast and followed the rail line back to Celle and made an uneventful landing."[5]

While some of the British pilots complained of the American pilots' chitchat on the radio, one exchange indicates that sometimes humor broke up the drudgery of flying the Airlift. A Tempelhof ground controller told a U. S. pilot that he was a minute ahead of schedule and to execute

► Nothing beats that hot cup of cocoa or coffee at Tempelhof Airfield, West Berlin. 1st Lt. John R. Oberschmid and his crew talk over the GCA landing that they just made at Tempelhof Airfield. As soon as their plane was unloaded, they quickly returned to Wiesbaden for another load of vital supplies. The mobile snack bar cut their ground time to a minimum. USAF NATIONAL MUSEUM

a 360-degree turn before landing. "A three-sixty will take me two minutes," the pilot said. There was a slight pause and the controller answered: "OK, do a one-eighty and back in."[6]

Newcomer pilots often were given a rough time on their first flight as this exchange between a pilot and the control tower shows: "BW 17 over Braunschweig at 05 at 7,000 feet upside down in a thunderstorm. What do I do now–over?" A new voice came on. "Now listen closely son. Over your head there is a little switch marked 'Inverter.' Take your right hand off the wheel and reach up and move that switch to the rear position and when the red light next to that switch goes out, you will be flying right side up and then you go to Rhein-Main–out."[7]

The men who flew for the Berlin Airlift risked their lives and health delivering food and supplies to people who had once been their enemy. Yet they did it the spirit of freedom and good will. Famous Candy Bomber and veteran pilot Gail Halvorsen recalled a conversation with his co-pilot. "One of my fellow Airlift pilots had bombed Berlin during the war. I asked him how he felt about flying day and night on behalf of the enemy, the very ones who did their best to kill him as he flew over Berlin in 1944. He hesitated a moment, shuffling his feet and then said, "It feels a lot better to feed them than it does to kill 'em." I only knew of one person who complained of flying day and night in behalf of the former enemy. This I believe was

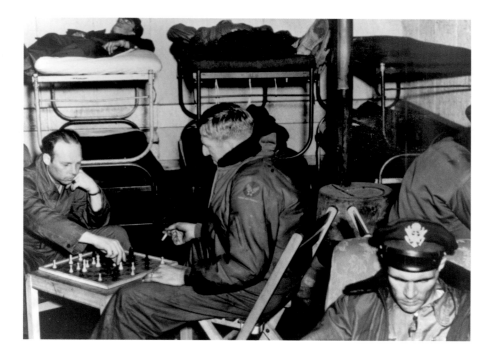

because of the overt expression of gratitude by the West Berliners. Everyone feels peace in their heart when they serve others. This was the case even though the "others" were the former enemy."[8]

ENDNOTES

1. Richard Reeves, *Daring Young Men*, p. 49

2. J. Sutherland & D. Canwell, *The Berlin Airlift*, p. 99

3. Die Berliner Luftbrücke Website

4. Thomas Parrish, *Berlin In The Balance*, p. 292

5. Ibid.

6. Ibid. p. 144

7. D. Giangreco and Robert Griffin, *Airbridge to Berlin*, p. 100-101

8. Berlin Brigade Website

◄ RAF pilots take a break from flying at a YMCA Canteen. Date and location unknown.
© ALLIIERTENMUSEUM / BERLIN

▲ Commonwealth pilots enjoy a break during Happy Hour at an undisclosed airbase.
COURTESY RICHARD ASH

▲ This young German served as a courier for the RAF pilots during the Berlin Airlift. Date and location unknown.
© AlliiertenMuseum / Berlin

▶ This mobile radar unit at Great Falls, Montana, was used to train pilots in the use of GCA approaches before they were assigned to the Berlin Airlift. NARA

▲ In a flight simulator at Great Falls, Montana in 1948, a pilot practices Tempelhof approaches. Soon he would be flying the Berlin Airlift.
NARA

◄ This mobile radar unit at Great Falls, Montana, was used to train airlift pilots in the use of GCA (ground controlled approach) approaches before they participated in the Berlin Airlift.
NATIONAL ARCHIVES

▼ At Rhein-Main Airfield, Navy and Air Force flight crews were briefed together for the day's missions to West Berlin.
USAF National Museum

▼ ▶ At Wiesbaden Air Force Base, Germany—Airlift pilots study a map of West Berlin to determine dropping points for the hundreds of candy bars parachuted to children in the blockaded city every day. Capt. Lawrence Caskey, left, explains the situation to Capt. Eugene Williams.
NARA

◀ A postcard from Great Falls, Montana where pilots received their final training before flying the Berlin Airlift.
Author's Collection

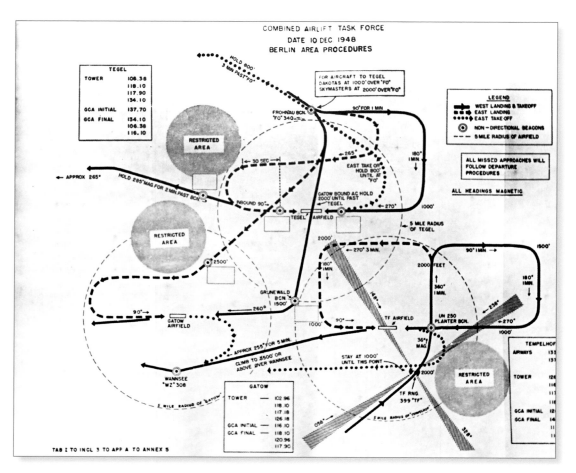

▲ This Berlin Area Procedures chart shows how intricate traffic patterns were during the Berlin Airlift.

▶ This parachute was specially made for "Vittles," a dog that flew 131 missions with his owner, 1st Lieutenant Russ Steber, during the Berlin Airlift. General Curtis LeMay named the dog "Vittles" and ordered a parachute made for him. Vittles, a boxer, accumulated around 2,000 flying hours, but never had to use the parachute. His owner, Lieutenant Steber, did have to bail out of a C-47 over the Soviet zone on one occasion, but Vittles was not with him on that trip. Steber was captured and returned to the West a few days later.

Lt Steber and "Vittles"

Berlin Airlift Dog Parachute
This parachute was specially made for "Vittles," a dog that flew 131 missions with his owner, 1st Lt Russ Steber, during the Berlin Airlift. General Curtis LeMay named the dog and ordered the parachute made for him. Vittles, a Boxer, accumulated around 2,000 flying hours, but never had to use the parachute. His owner, Lt Steber, did have to bail out of a C-47 over the Soviet zone on one occasion, but Vittles was not with him on that trip. Steber was captured and returned to the West a few days later.

Vittles' story was an interesting and light-hearted news item during the Berlin Airlift. These photos appeared in many newspapers.

539,112 AND THE LAST TON OF COAL FROM FASSBERG

▲ Major Bill Anderson examines damage on his C-54 after a runaway prop destroyed the rear part of the cockpit.
AUTHOR'S COLLECTION

◀ In 1949, a C-54, its crew, and British officers celebrate the last load of coal from Fassberg to West Berlin. |
NARA

◄ As the first phase of the Berlin Airlift was celebrated, nine-year-old Suzanna Joks of West Berlin presented a bouquet of flowers to Lieutenant Donald W. Measley of Hampton, New Jersey.
AUTHOR'S COLLECTION

▶ After the Berlin Airlift, trains out of the West Berlin rotating military personnel home were often covered with colorful military graffiti.
NARA

◄◄ A C-54 Skymaster on final approach to Tempelhof Airfield, Berlin, 1948. "If you landed on the left runway, you came down between buildings over a graveyard...chop off your power, push the yoke forward, pull it back, and you were on the ground. If you missed your approach, you did not go around but flew back to Frankfurt, landed, got back in line, and flew to Berlin again." (Mark Taylor, U.S. Navy pilot)
USAF NATIONAL MUSEUM

◄ On April 7, 1949, fog clears and light-lined runway appears ahead. Approach to Tempelhof runway is between two rows of jagged buildings with graveyard in center.
NARA

► (Overleaf) In 1948, a C-54 Skymaster landing at Tempelhof Airfield, West Berlin.
NARA

4. UPGRADING THE AIRFIELDS

A s the Berlin Airlift moved into its third month of operation it became obvious that there were not enough ground facilities to handle the air traffic into the three Allied Airfields in West Berlin. Tempelhof could not expand beyond the three runways

it had, and the third was still under construction. Gatow, in the British sector, did not have room to expand. But Tegel, in the French sector, lent itself to expansion. The terrain around Tegel was unobstructed except for a Russian controlled radio tower. And it had nearby rail and road access.

The French quickly agreed to maintain a new airfield if the U. S. would build it. Normally, runways were built with a minimum two-foot foundation, using concrete. But there wasn't any available in Berlin at that time. The problem was solved by recycling brick from all of the bombed out buildings in West Berlin.

Cobblestones and gravel used as ballast from railway tracks in Berlin were also supplied and run through crushers. "When the track ballast was used, the Russians who operated the railroads in Berlin yelled to high heaven, but it did them no good."[1] After World War II, as reparations, the Russians had taken most of Berlin's rolling stock and railway tracks back to Russia. It was sweet revenge for the Berlin laborers to remove the gravel used for railroad ties.

The next challenge was to move construction equipment into Berlin. The largest U.S. aircraft, the C-74, could not accommodate bulky tractors and graders. So the equipment was cut into pieces at Rhein-Main and then reassembled after the C-74s delivered them to Berlin.

Soon some 17,000 Berliners worked around the clock in three eight-hour shifts to build the main runway in a record three months. Hot meals were supplied for each shift and women comprised almost half of the work force. The project

consumed the equivalent of 10 city blocks of brick, and tests showed that the new runway was stronger than the average runway in the United States.

The only hitch in completing the new Tegel Airfield was the 200-foot radio tower that belonged to Soviet controlled East Berlin. After diplomats could not get the Russians to dismantle the tower, the French took matters into their own

▲ During the Airlift, these high intensity runway lights at Tempelhof Airfield were turned on when the visibility dropped to 1/8 of a mile. They were useful to pilots transitioning from the GCA approach guidance to the landing phase of their flights.
AUTHOR'S COLLECTION

▲ During the Berlin Airlift these parallel rows of high intensity lights made landings easier at Tempelhof Airport. The left row, as seen by the pilot on final, was red and the right row yellow. This display indicated that he was on the correct glideslope. During daylight, some pilots used this system to land when the visibility was less than 500 feet. NARA

▶ Aerial of Tempelhof Airport, West Berlin, 1948. At the time, it appears there was only one paved runway. USAF NATIONAL MUSEUM

◄ This rock crusher was cut into pieces, airlifted into West Berlin, and finally reassembled for building two new runways at Tempelhof Airfield. NARA

hands. Brigadier General Jean Ganeval ordered a platoon of French Army engineers to blow up the tower. The Russians bitterly complained but the tower was gone. "When the Soviet Commandant Kotikov, said: 'How could you do such a thing?' Ganeval replied; 'With the help of dynamite and French sappers."[2]

Under the RAF, Gatow Airfield ran like a Swiss watch. However, when migrating birds interfered with operations at Gatow, a sharp RAF officer dreamed up a simple solution. He dispatched an aircraft to Malta to bring back some hungry falcons. Immediately, the problem was solved and migrating birds avoided Gatow.

Humor could surface in ground operations. Sometimes irreverent American radio calls woke up British controllers with an entertaining report:

"Here comes a Yankee
With a blackened soul
Heading for Gatow
With a load of coal."[3]

Tempelhof Airfield also needed some upgrading–it had only one runway when the Airlift began and by the time Tegel was under construction, it had two and a partial third. So some of the equipment flown in for Tegel Airfield was also used to improve and complete Tempelhof's runways. Landings at Tempelhof Airfield were quite challenging because of the proximity of high apartment buildings to the main runway. "GCA equipment had to be positioned at the end of the runway farthest from the approaching aircraft, so

◄ High intensity approach lights were installed at the Tempelhof Airfield in straight rows, marking the extensions of the runway. Extensive tests with the ASA lights were made at Landing Aids Experiments Station, Arcata, California. Some aircraft landed when visibility limits were one-sixteenth of a mile. PSP (perforated steel planking) usually used for runway and taxiway reinforcement, also was used for these light towers.
NARA

that the radar could see over the buildings. Most pilots came in high and had to be coaxed down by the GCA controllers. Because of this psychological hazard no aircraft was ever wrecked by landing too short at Tempelhof, but landing too far down the runway wrecked three."[4] High intensity approach lighting was also installed at the graveyard located near the approach end of the main runway. The Russians claimed that the graveyard was being desecrated as some graves were being be relocated. Berliners ignored the propaganda and fully endorsed the project.

ENDNOTES

1 Aviation Operations Magazine, *A Special Study of Operation Vittles*, p. 61

2 J. Sutherland & D. Canwell, *The Berlin Airlift*, p.115

3 *Air Force Magazine*, October 1998, Inside the Berlin Airlift

4 J. Sutherland & D. Canwell, *The Berlin Airlift*, p. 111

▲ In 1948, these bulldozers graded a new runway at Tempelhof Airfield. After dozing the rubble, tar was applied, and finally steel matting.
NARA

► Laborers
install
Marston
(PSP) matting
for a new
runway at
Tempelhof
Airfield.
NARA

▲ In September 1948, construction of Tegel Airfield was well underway. Here, a bulldozer is working on a taxiway.
NARA

◄ Empty asphalt barrels line the 6,000-foot airstrip at the new Tegel Airfield in the French Sector of Berlin. Date unknown.
USAF NATIONAL MUSEUM

▲ A view of West Berlin's Tegel airport in the French zone in June 1948. Built in ninety days, the Tegel airfield was, at that time, the largest airport of the world. In this area were two radio towers (reportedly approximately 80 and 120 meters in height) belonging to Soviet-controlled Radio Berlin. These towers made the approach to the new Tegel airfield unacceptably dangerous. Prior to Tegel's completion, French General Ganeval had asked the Soviets to remove or relocate the towers. The Soviets had refused. Ganeval then advised the Soviets that if the towers were not removed, he would remove them. Still the Soviets did nothing. Ganeval was a man of his word. On December 16, 1948, at approximately 1100 hours, local time, on his order, French sappers used explosives to demolish the two towers blocking the approach to Tegel airfield. The Soviets were outraged. Ganeval's Soviet counterpart, Lieutenant General Alexander Kotikov, called Ganeval and reportedly asked him how he could possibly have done this. Ganeval was reported to have said, "With dynamite of course."
USAF

◄ In 1948, over 17,000 West Berliners completed the 6,000-foot runway at Tegel Airfield in the French Sector. It could handle the largest aircraft in the Berlin Airlift.
AUTHOR'S COLLECTION

► The first C-54 about to land at the new Tegel Airfield on November 5, 1948.
USAF NATIONAL MUSEUM

▼ In March 1949, construction of an unloading ramp is well underway at Tegel Airfield in the French Sector of West Berlin.
NARA

► An aerial view of Tegel Airfield in November 1948. Note the Soviet radio tower upper left that was later demolished by the French Army when the Soviets refused to dismantle it.
AUTHOR'S COLLECTION

▼ Steamrollers crush rubble for a new runway at the Gatow Airfield in the British sector. In the background, a C-47 is landing with its priceless cargo.
AUTHOR'S COLLECTION

►► In 1948, the British installed underground fuel tanks at Gatow Airfield to expedite aircraft unloading fuel supplies for West Berliners. A pipeline then carried oil to tanker barges for transport to central Berlin.
AUTHOR'S COLLECTION

▲ Marston matting, sometimes known as PSP, helped strengthen upgraded runways and taxiways during the Airlift. Here it is being installed at Gatow Airfield in Berlin.

© AllⅡertenMuseum / Berlin

▶ RAF Yorks and U.S. C-54 Skymasters at Gatow Airfield in the British sector. Date unknown.

USAF National Museum

▲ U. S. C-54 Skymasters being unloaded at Gatow Airfield in the British Sector. Date unknown. USAF
NATIONAL MUSEUM

▲ Ten Avro York aircraft unloading supplies at RAF Gatow Airfield.

◄ At Wunstorf Airfield in West Germany, unloading Airlift supplies from a train for shipment to West Berlin in 1948. In the background, an Avro York is about to touch down. AUTHOR'S COLLECTION

▲ In October 1948, over a dozen C-54s and a few C-47s await cargo at Rhein-Main Airfield. Note the hastily constructed tents in foreground. AUTHOR'S COLLECTION

▲ In March 1949, C-54s stand out against the snow
at Wiesbaden Air Base during the Berlin Airlift.

Courtesy of U.S. Army Garrison Wiesbaden

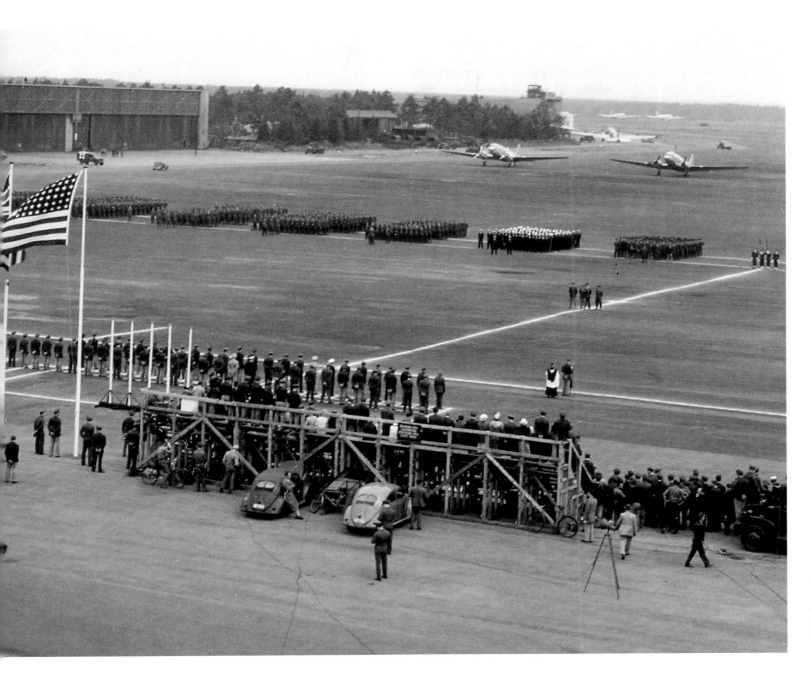

◄ On July 29, 1949, the
Allies put on a military
parade at Fassberg
Airfield in the British zone
celebrating its contribution
to the Airlift.
NARA

5. SUPPLYING THE WEST BERLINERS

Once the Allies decided to challenge Stalin and support the two and one-half million West Berliners, challenges for the Airlift became immense. It was the only way to transport food and supplies to the city. The daily food requirements for West Berlin were: 646 tons of flour and wheat, 125 tons of cereal, 64 tons of

◄ In 1949, currency reform enabled these housewives in the Western sector of Berlin to shop for and purchase food items they sorely missed during the early months of the Airlift.

► Frau Marta Pallmayer of the Neuköln neighborhood collecting her weekly coal ration during the Berlin Airlift.
USAF NATIONAL MUSEUM

Because of the cutoff of electricity from East Berlin and gas rationing, West Berliners also had to put up with reduced transportation schedules–subways, buses, and streetcars operated on limited timetables. Many factories and offices also had to be shut down. But Berliners had grown accustomed to rationing and shortages during six long years of war and three years of occupation.

A young American enlisted man dreamed up a bold way to get fuel to Berlin homes. "A seventeen-year-old corporal, Louis Schuerholz, of Ocean City, Maryland, described one incident this way: "We were assigned to neighborhoods to deliver food and fuel to German homes… on one occasion, we drove into East Berlin and approached a Russian fuel dump. We had some Four Roses whiskey, got the guards drunk and took 5,000 gallons of fuel oil which

fats, 109 tons of meat and fish, 180 tons of dehydrated potatoes, 85 tons of sugar, 11 tons of coffee, 19 tons of dry skimmed milk, 5 tons of whole milk for children, 3 tons of yeast for baking, 144 tons of dehydrated vegetables, 38 tons of salt, and 10 tons of cheese. "Everything Berlin got – came in by air. You can't begin to imagine how much aspirin, how many rolls of toilet paper, how much salt and pepper two and a half million people consume every day."[1]

we then delivered to German households in our assigned neighborhoods."[2]

Most of the food shipped into Berlin was dehydrated to keep aircraft payloads manageable. But open land in West Berlin, such as the Tiergarten, was turned into vegetable gardens, and thousands of the park's trees were cut down for firewood. Airlift aircraft were "landing or taking off from West Berlin's two Airfields every thirty seconds, day and night...Most of this [the supplies] was food and coal, but also included cargo like food for the animals in the Berlin Zoo, chocolate for Christmas, paper for the newspapers, seedlings to replace the trees that had been cut down, even Volkswagen cars for the Berlin Police."[3]

In hopes of foiling the Allies' attempts to rebuild Berlin, the Soviets invited West Berliners to cross into the Soviet Zone and register for food and fuel rations, but few took advantage of this Russian ploy. In December of 1948, West Berliners ignored the Russians' offer and in a citywide vote, rejected the Communists and supported their own parties.

ENDNOTES

1 Lt. Col. Harold Watson / Die Berliner Luftbrücke Website
2 Richard Reeves, *Daring Young Men*, p. 223
3 Serge Schmemann / Die Berliner Luftbrücke Website

◀ During the blockade, West Berliners had their own gardens to supplement what food the Airlift could supply. This one was near the Brandenburg Gate.
LANDESARCHIV BERLIN

◀ In West Germany, two women are processing dehydrated potatoes for shipment to West Berlin.
© BUNDESARCHIV

◀ In West Berlin as the Airlift began, this nun helped remove debris from the Hedwigskirche cathedral after the Bishop of Berlin asked for volunteers.
AUTHOR'S COLLECTION

▲ During the Airlift, a West Berliner in her bathing suit puts in time rebuilding a road. Such laborers were given additional rations for their efforts.
AUTHOR'S COLLECTION

▶ In 1947, students were rebuilding Berlin's Technical University with help from West Berlin's military governments, the Quakers, and the British Red Cross.
AUTHOR'S COLLECTION

◄ See previous caption.

▼ West Berlin kids get a soup break during the Airlift. Date unknown.
AUTHOR'S COLLECTION

► In West Berlin, forty abandoned barges dominated this harbor after their owners left them due to continued Soviet interference with barge traffic. Date unknown.
AUTHOR'S COLLECTION

◄◄ With an Airlift aircraft arriving in West Berlin every few minutes, pedestrians took them for granted as they went about their business.
AUTHOR'S COLLECTION

◄ In 1948, West Berlin kids made a playground out of the remains of a zoo-bunker near the Tiergarten.
AUTHOR'S COLLECTION

► West Berlin youngsters who lived near the Tempelhof Airfield play at a game called "Luftbrücke" (air bridge). The children used model American planes that were sold in German toy shops throughout the western sector of Berlin.
AUTHOR'S COLLECTION

◀ West Berlin children being evacuated in C-47s to West Germany from West Berlin's Tempelhof Airport in the early stages of the Airlift. USAF NATIONAL MUSEUM

▶ West Berlin children were often ferried out of West Berlin to West Germany in empty Airlift aircraft when rationing got tough. Allied personnel often hosted them when they arrived in West Germany. USAF NATIONAL MUSEUM

◄ During holidays, children often went from West Berlin by bus or aircraft to West Germany where they could get more food.
USAF National Museum

► Often children from West Berlin were flown into West Germany for holidays. This sergeant and his wife hosted a young West Berliner. Date unknown.
Author's Collection

▲ This ad promoted one of the benefits of the Airlift – milk for West Berlin children.

▲ Often West German orphans were sent packages of food and clothing from the United States.

► Schoolrooms were often without heat, so students and teachers came to school wearing overcoats.

◀ In "Operation Little Vittles," this U. S. Air Force C-74 brought gifts all the way from the United States to the West Berlin children during Christmas. NARA

▲ In December 1948, the U.S. Air Force implemented "Operation Santa Claus" and delivered packages of clothing, candy, and toys to West Berlin children. This flight alone delivered more than twenty thousand Christmas presents. Author's Collection

◄ This operation, codenamed "Camel Caravan" delivered 5,000 pounds of food, candy, books, and games to West Berlin for distribution to children during the Berlin Airlift. The camel was acquired while the fighter squadron was in Tripoli, Libya, and his name was Clarence. He went to West Berlin to cheer up the children.
AUTHOR'S COLLECTION

► This camel was a hit with West Berlin kids–he brought them Christmas presents from the United States and West Germany.
© ALLIIERTENMUSEUM / BERLIN

▼ Bob Hope struggles through a crowd upon his arrival in West Berlin during the Airlift.
© AlliiertenMuseum / Berlin

▲ Montgomery Clift and Paul Douglas starred in this 1950 re-enactment of the Berlin Airlift. BIG LIFT is about enlisted men falling in love with West German women after World War II, while they are doing their duty as airmen. Much of the movie was filmed on location in Berlin. With the exception of Montgomery Clift and Paul Douglas, all military personnel appearing in this film were actual members of the U.S. Armed Forces on duty in Germany.
© Twentieth Century Fox Film Corporation

◄ ◄ West Berlin children receiving Christmas presents in December 1948.
Author's Collection

◄ Bob Hope on arrival at Tempelhof Airfield in 1956 for the Berlin Film Festival. He also visited West Berlin during the Berlin Airlift to cheer up the Allied Forces and West Berliners.
Author's Collection

6. THE CANDY BOMBER

During this tough time for the West Berliners, a human angel, Lieutenant Gail Halvorsen, came to the rescue. This veteran U. S. Air Force pilot devised candy parachutes for West Berlin children and as he regularly landed at Tempelhof Airfield, he would wiggle his C-54's wings to alert

◀ A C-54 Skymaster drops candy bars as it prepares to land at Tempelhof Airfield,
USAF

▶ 1st Lieutenant Gail S. Halvorsen of the 17th Military Air Transport Squadron rigs up some candy bars to miniature parachutes for delivery to West Berlin children. His unusual project became known as "Operation Little Vittles" and he became a celebrity. The West Berliners gave him a nickname—the Candy Bomber.
NARA

◀ In 1949, a group of West Berlin children express their appreciation to Lt. Gail Halvorsen, the originator of "Operation Little Vittles", for the thousands of packages of gum and candy he and fellow Airlift pilots delivered to them by parachute. NARA

▶ In "Operation Little Vittles" pilots dropped tiny parachutes with candy to West Berlin children. In this picture, a pilot tosses candy to eager children after landing at Tempelhof Airfield. NARA

▲ Children flocked to Tempelhof Airfield in anticipation of candy drops by incoming U.S. Airlift aircraft.
AUTHOR'S COLLECTION

◀ As the Candy Bomber, Lt. Gail Halvorsen, increased his candy drops to 1500 per day, he recruited a secretary and translator to help him answer the huge amount of incoming mail from West Berlin children. NARA

the children that he was going to drop candy on final approach. When his superiors learned of this operation, they eventually endorsed it. Soon, candy companies and individuals in West Germany began supplying plenty of treats for the hungry children, and Lieutenant Halvorsen became known as The Candy Bomber.

"One day in July 1948 I met 30 kids at the barbed wire fence at Tempelhof in Berlin. They were excited. They said, "When the weather gets so bad you can't land don't worry about us. We can get by on little food but if we lose our freedom we may never get it back." The principle of freedom was more important than the pleasure of enough flour. "Just don't give up on us," they asked. The Soviets had offered the Berliners food rations but they would not

capitulate. For the hour I was at the fence not one child asked for gum or candy. Children I had met during and after the war like them in other countries had always begged insistently for such treasures. These Berlin children were so grateful for flour they wouldn't lower themselves to be beggars for something more. It was even the more impressive because they hadn't had gum or candy for months. When I realized this silent, mature show of gratitude and the strength that it took not to ask, I had to do something. All I had was two sticks of gum. I broke them in two and passed them through the barbed wire. The result was unbelievable. Those with the gum tore off strips of the wrapper and gave them to the others. Those with the strips put them to their noses and smelled the tiny fragrance. The

▲ At approach end of main
Tempelhof runway, West
Berlin kids await a Halvorsen
candy drop.
NARA

expression of pleasure was immeasurable. I was so moved
by what I saw and their incredible restraint that I promised
them I would drop enough gum for each of them the next
day as I came over their heads to land. They would know

my plane because I would wiggle the wings as I came over
the airport. When I got back to Rhein-Main I attached gum
and even chocolate bars to three handkerchief parachutes.
We wiggled the wings and delivered the goods the next

day. What a jubilant celebration. We did the same thing for several weeks before we got caught, threatened with a court martial which was followed by a sudden pardon." General Tunner said, "Keep it up."[1]

"In 1998 on a visit to Berlin flying an old Airlift C-54, *The Spirit of Freedom*, with Tim Chopp, a 60-year-old man told me he had caught a parachute in 1948. "It had a fresh Hershey candy bar attached. It took me a week to eat it," he said. "I hid it day and night. But it was not the chocolate that was most important. The most important was that someone in America knew I was in trouble and someone cared. That was hope for me." And then, with moist eyes, he said, "Without hope the soul dies. I can live on thin rations but not without hope." That is what the British, French and American Berlin Airlift, its dried eggs, dried potatoes, dried milk and coal meant to the Berliners: hope for freedom. There is a universal need for hope today every bit as much now as it was needed then. Airlift is supplying hope around the world today, as it did in Berlin – to the unfortunate who are oppressed by man or nature.

My experience on the Airlift taught me that gratitude, hope, and service before self can bring happiness to the soul when the opposite brings despair. Because not one of 30 children begged for chocolate, thousands of children in Berlin received over 20 tons of chocolate, gum, and goodies dropped from C-54 Skymasters over a 14-month period."[2]

ENDNOTES

1 Berlin Brigade Website

2 German Mission to the United States

◀ Retired Colonel Gail Halverson demonstrates the handkerchief parachutes he used to drop candy to the German children during "Operation Vittles." He has returned to Berlin numerous times since the Airlift and received many honors from the German government and the US Air Force. USAF

7. THE AIRCRAFT

n 1948, the Berlin Blockade caught the Allies by surprise. But thanks to President Harry

Truman's commitment to jump-starting the Airlift and getting experienced officers to

run it, there always existed a critical element—hope. The Berliners and the Allies also did

◄◄ A Douglas C-54 Skymaster, the workhorse of the Berlin Airlift. USAF

▲ C-47 Skytrains were in high demand in the early stages of the Berlin Airlift . The British also contributed their C-47 Dakotas to the effort. AUTHOR'S COLLECTION

A U.S. Air Force C-74 Globemaster delivers 25 tons of flour to Gatow Airport in the British sector of West Berlin during the Airlift. It was the largest single load to be airlifted into West Berlin, and Gatow Airport was used because at that time it had the longest runway in the Western sector.
IMPERIAL WAR MUSEUM

Cockpit of the Navy MATS R-5D. The Navy contributed two squadrons of R-5Ds to the Airlift. It was the Navy version of the C-54.
U.S. NAVY

Master Sergeant William Gillian was chief engineer on this first C-74 Globemaster flight into Rhein-Main Airfield in August, 1948. Subsequently, it carried much heavy equipment into West Berlin. Passageways were provided in the wing to permit the flight engineer to perform servicing and repairs while the C-74 was in flight.
NARA

their part. Initially, the U.S. and British could only gather the available DC-3s and C-47s that were scattered all over Europe. But these reliable aircraft could not move the volume of coal and food necessary to keep West Berlin going.

There was a solution. "The DC-3's big sister, the four-engine Douglas DC-4 (known in the U.S. Air Force as the C-54 or in the U.S. Navy as the R-5D) could carry fifty-five passengers–or ten tons of cargo, more than three times the capacity of the C-47 (its civilian version was the famous DC-3). But only two of the Air Force's four hundred C-54s were in Germany. Most were thousands of miles away, transporting men and supplies from country to country, island to island across the Pacific Ocean…One group, twelve planes, was based in Guam, more than 3,800 miles west of Hawaii and more than 11,000 miles from Germany."[1]

▲ In 1948, the first C-74 Globemaster used in the Berlin Airlift delivered 20 tons of flour to Gatow Airfield in the British sector. It made the trip from Frankfurt in one hour and seven minutes. AUTHOR'S COLLECTION

▶ A Lockheed C-121G Super Constellation was even recruited for the Berlin Airlift. AUTHOR'S COLLECTION

In addition to the C-47s and the C-54s, the U.S. Air Force supplied one Douglas C-74 Globemaster I, five Fairchild C-82 Packets, and at the very end of the Airlift, one Boeing C-97 Stratofreighter. Initially the C-74 carried foodstuffs but later was used to carry C-54 engines from the United States to Germany. It had a payload of 48,000 pounds and a range of 1,500 statute miles.

The C-82s ferried a variety of equipment into Berlin: graders, ambulances, snowplows, jeeps, and power station parts. Often its rear doors were removed before Airlift flights to allow for unusually bulky loads. It had a payload of 12,000 pounds and a range of 500 statute miles.

Though the C-97 joined the Airlift as late as May 1949, "it did play a part, psychologically as well as practically... Had the Airlift continued, 52 Stratofreighters could have carried the same load into Berlin as 240 C-54s."[2] It had a payload of 53,000 pounds and a range of 1,500 statute miles. The British supplied a variety of aircraft for the Airlift – over a dozen – each with different capabilities. The Short Sunderland, with a big payload, could land on one of West Berlin's lakes or rivers until freeze-up and the Lancastrian tankers could deliver avgas (aviation gasoline) for the Airlift aircraft. The biggest problem was upgrading airfields in West Berlin and West Germany to accommodate the huge number of military and civilian aircraft.

Eventually seven RAF squadrons operated from Lübeck Airfield, north of Hamburg, and they brought in coal, newsprint, materials, and equipment to keep West Berlin's industries afloat.

► Towards the end of the Berlin Airlift the U.S. Air Force used a Boeing YC-97A Stratofreighter similar to this one, as well as a C-74 Globemaster, testing the feasibility of heavy-lift transports and their use in a prolonged operation. The plan was to use C-97s and 124s to continue the operation with much bigger payloads, cutting down the number of flights required.
COURTESY BERLIN AIRLIFT HISTORICAL FOUNDATION

► The Fairchild C-82 Packet, the forerunner of the C-119 Flying Boxcar, was used in the Berlin Airlift for heavy hauling. It was especially useful for moving oversized and bulky equipment into West Berlin for upgrading and building airfields.
USAF

►► (Facing page) A U.S. Air Force C-82 Packet freighter landing at Tempelhof during the Berlin Airlift.
AUTHOR'S COLLECTION

ENDNOTES
1   Richard Reeves, *Daring Young Men*, p. 40
2   J. Provan & R. Davies, *Berlin Airlift*, p. 28
3   J. Sutherland & D. Canwell, *Berlin Airlift*, p. 59

▲ (Both photos) An ambulance is unloaded from a U. S. Air Force C-82 Packet at Tempelhof Airfield. There was a serious shortage of hospital equipment in West Berlin during the Airlift. AUTHOR'S COLLECTION

"The first British civilian charter flight came from Bückeburg into Gatow on 27 July. Elsewhere there had been tremendous progress and transport aircraft were actually far outstripping the facilities at Wunstorf. Consequently, all of the RAF and civilian C-47s were moved out to Fassburg on 29 July. Four-engine civilian aircraft remained at Wunstorf, along with the RAF's own Avro Yorks."[3]

▶ Flight Refueling Limited had a fleet of Avro Lancastrians that carried more than 27,000 tons of petroleum fuel into West Berlin – almost a third of the total required. This workhorse had four Rolls-Royce 1,750 horsepower Merlin 85 engines. AUTHOR'S COLLECTION

◄ An Avro Lancaster, similar to this one, was converted to a tanker, and delivered over 221 tons of fuel to West Berlin. Unfortunately, it later crashed en route to its home base in the United Kingdom with a loss of eight souls.

AUTHOR'S COLLECTION

▲ The Short S-25 Sunderland was a British flying boat patrol bomber developed for the Royal Air Force (RAF). Based on the S-23 Empire flying boat, the flagship of Imperial Airways, the S-25 was re-engineered for military service and was used in the Berlin Airlift for carrying coal. The Sunderlands operated from Finkenwerder, Hamburg, landing on Lake Havel in West Berlin. They flew until winter icing rendered the lake too hazardous for seaplane operations.

AUTHOR'S COLLECTION

◄ In 1948, An RAF Sunderland of the 201st Squadron unloads its cargo on Lake Havel.
USAF National Museum

► On the Havel River in West Berlin, two boats prepare to unload coal from an RAF Sunderland Flying Boat.
Author's Collection

▲ With a payload of 20,500 pounds, the Avro York comprised close to two thirds of the RAF's contribution to the Berlin Airlift. 35 Avro Yorks participated in the Airlift.
AUTHOR'S COLLECTION

▶ The York transport aircraft did significant work in the Berlin Airlift and later had some success as a civilian airliner. It was derived from the Lancaster bomber; fortunately for the passengers the fuselage was redesigned and much more spacious.
COURTESY RAF

◄ Scottish Airlines supplied a converted civilian version of this Consolidated B-24 Liberator to the Berlin Airlift. It carried fuel to West Berlin. USAF

► The Handley Page Hastings was rushed into service with the onset of the Berlin Airlift, flying its first sortie to West Berlin on November 11, 1948. The Hastings fleet was mainly used to carry coal, delivering 55,000 tons. AUTHOR'S COLLECTION

◄ Civilian operators used Handley Page Halifax surplus bombers to haul freight and diesel fuel to the besieged city. The Halifax's that the B.O.A.C. Airways had converted for civilian use were named Halifax Haltons. AUTHOR'S COLLECTION

◄ The B.S.A.A. (British South American Airways) Avro Tudors proved to be valuable workhorses for the Berlin Airlift. They could carry 2,000 gallons of diesel fuel – a scarce commodity in West Berlin. To access the cockpit, the pilots climbed in through a roof hatch. The Tudors could also carry up to 9 tons of cargo on non-fuel flights. AUTHOR'S COLLECTION

► Four Bristol 170 Freighters, operated by Silver City Airways, participated in the Berlin Airlift. They were part of the 104 civilian aircraft that participated. Some were on scheduled services into West Berlin. AUTHOR'S COLLECTION

◀ The Bristol 170 Freighter Mk21 was a valuable
contribution to the Airlift with its huge nose doors.
It had a payload of 8,700 pounds.
© AlliiertenMuseum / Berlin

▲ Because of their commitment to troops in Indo China, the French did not
have many aircraft to support the Airlift. But they did supply three Junkers
52 aircraft that operated out of Wunstorf, like this restored German model.
Unfortunately, two of the Junkers crashed into each other during the Airlift.
Author's Collection

8. MAINTENANCE

An aircraft supplying Berlin could be flown by a crew of three. It needed at least

a further seven men to keep it fit to fly and ideally each aircraft would have a

maintenance crew of fifteen. . . . Some of the aircraft, like the C-47s and their British

At Celle Airfield in West Germany, Allied C-54s await maintenance before returning to Airlift duties.
IMPERIAL WAR MUSEUM

Aerial photograph of RAF Station Celle during the Berlin Airlift. It was a key maintenance base for the Airlift.
AUTHOR'S COLLECTION

cousins the Dakotas, were obsolete, the Hastings was so new that its needs could not be foreseen; neither the old nor the new had adequate reserves of spare parts…Their engines, built for long periods of cruising, were pounded by constant high-manifold pressure and heavy revving. Their airframes were strained by the weight of cargo and repeated landings fully laden which also overtaxed hydraulics, brake discs and cables."[1]

German-speaking officers were found to superintend them, manuals were translated and the result was high class work and the release of USAF men for other jobs."[2]

As the workhorse of the Berlin Airlift, the U. S. Air Force's Skymaster C-54 and its Navy counterpart, the R-5D, required the most maintenance of any aircraft. Drawing from bases as far away as Guam and Alaska, the United States gathered 354 C-54 and R-5D aircraft for use in the Airlift. But to keep 128 active, carrying supplies to Berlin, over 200 aircraft were always down for maintenance in West Germany, the United Kingdom, and the United States.

The C-54s were carrying heavier loads than the aircraft were designed for and landing at glide angles made for hard landings. Tempelhof was a case in point. Coal was a messy cargo and caused numerous maintenance problems. "One veteran C-54 radio operator, Lloyd Banquer, recalled seeing coal residue in his C-54 in Morocco some five years after the Airlift."[3] The RAF Sunderland seaplanes were much less vulnerable to corrosion problems but could not go into Berlin when the lakes froze up. The U. S. Air Force required 50-hour maintenance checks at the airbase from which the C-54s operated and work went on around the clock, seven days a week. After three 50 hour maintenance checks, the aircraft would then be flown to Burtonwood, England, for more extensive maintenance. On the fifth 50 hour maintenance deadline, the aircraft went all the way back to California, Texas, or New York, for a 1,000 hour inspection.

These requirements, in addition to unforeseen engine failures, crashes, and other unscheduled maintenance

Both the U.S. Air Force and the RAF had trouble keeping enough mechanics on duty. According to the Potsdam agreement before the Airlift, German labor could only be used for certain less skilled maintenance work on aircraft. But the U. S. Air Force looked the other way and "took on up to eighty-five German mechanics, mainly Luftwaffe trained, for each squadron's routine maintenance.

problems make it easy to understand why so many aircraft were required to move cargo into Berlin. All of these checks were coordinated through the use of control boards, at various airbases and headquarters, with colored markers. White = operational, Red = scheduled maintenance, Green = unscheduled maintenance, Yellow = in base shops for 3rd and 4th echelon maintenance, Blue = 200 hour inspection at Burtonwood, U.K., Black = Aircraft grounded for parts (AOCP).

During the Airlift, the Group Maintenance Officer, Major Vance Cornelius, of the 1442nd Squadron noted, "I see no difference between this and war time except that during the last portion of the war we had a good supply of spare parts salvaged from flak damaged planes. Here we have less."[4] Spark plugs and windshield wipers were a

▲ At Rhein-Main Airfield, a checker keeps a watchful eye on the supply of tires for the C-54 Berlin Airlift.
Thousands of tires, checked constantly for deterioration, were kept in a state of readiness for use in the Airlift.
USAF NATIONAL MUSEUM

▲ Mechanics of Royal Air Force Honington's central servicing unit replace the brake mechanism in the wheel of an Avro York transport aircraft.

IMPERIAL WAR MUSEUM

▲ Navy VR-6 mechanics change an R-5D tire as an Air Force corporal lends a helping hand.

USAF NATIONAL MUSEUM

Royal Air Force mechanics undertake engine and prop maintenance on a Dakota transport aircraft at RAF Lübeck, West Germany.
IMPERIAL WAR MUSEUM

▶▶ Night loading an RAF Dakota at Honington airfield, Suffolk. Rolls-Royce Merlin engines, wheels, and other spare parts are being loaded under mercury vapor lights, for transport to West Berlin.
IMPERIAL WAR MUSEUM

critical problem. "A supply of windshield wipers, estimated to last six months, was used up in two weeks. 60,000 spark plugs had to be reconditioned each month."[5]

The Royal Air Force had a different problem, keeping their aircraft in service. "Comparing the aircraft in terms of maintenance, it is easy to see why the Americans had a distinct advantage. After two hours' flying, the C-54 would need maintenance work taking up to an hour and a half. However an Avro York needed three hours of servicing for the same amount of flying time…the RAF over-inspected and over-repaired their aircraft. They allowed only thirty-six minor problems in an aircraft before it was handed over to maintenance, whereas the USAF allowed 350."[6]

They also had more than ten different kinds of aircraft supporting the Airlift. On the other hand, the British aircraft were only a short hop from their manufacturing and major overhaul facilities in the United Kingdom and they did not have as many aircraft to maintain as the U. S. forces.

The French Air Force could only supply a Junkers JU-52 and a few C-47s to Operation Vittles. With plenty of German aircraft mechanics available in West Berlin and West Germany, the JU-52 was relatively easy to maintain.

ENDNOTES

1 A. & J. Tusa, *The Berlin Airlift*, p. 309
2 Ibid. p. 311
3 Bruce McAllister Interview, 12/1/13
4 *A Special Study of "Operation Vittles"* By Aviation Operations Magazine, p.78
5 J. Provan & R. Davies, *Berlin Airlift*, p. 40
6 J. Sutherland & D. Canwell, *The Berlin Airlift*, p. 104

▲ Cleaning spare engine parts at Warrington-Burtonwood Air Depot, England. These mechanics are cleaning cylinder baffles. USAF

▶ WAAF (Women's Auxiliary Air Force) Corporal Margaret Fisher and another engineer working on an RAF Dakota.
© AlliiertenMuseum / Berlin

► Mechanics work on a Junkers
JU-52 aircraft at Tempelhof.
The French Air Force contributed
this aircraft to the Airlift.
© ALLIIERTENMUSEUM / BERLIN

◄ Engines were inspected and minor adjustments made during the unloading of aircraft at Tempelhof Airfield. NARA

▲ In 1948, a C-47 Skytrain undergoes minor engine repairs.

▲ Mechanic taking a break.

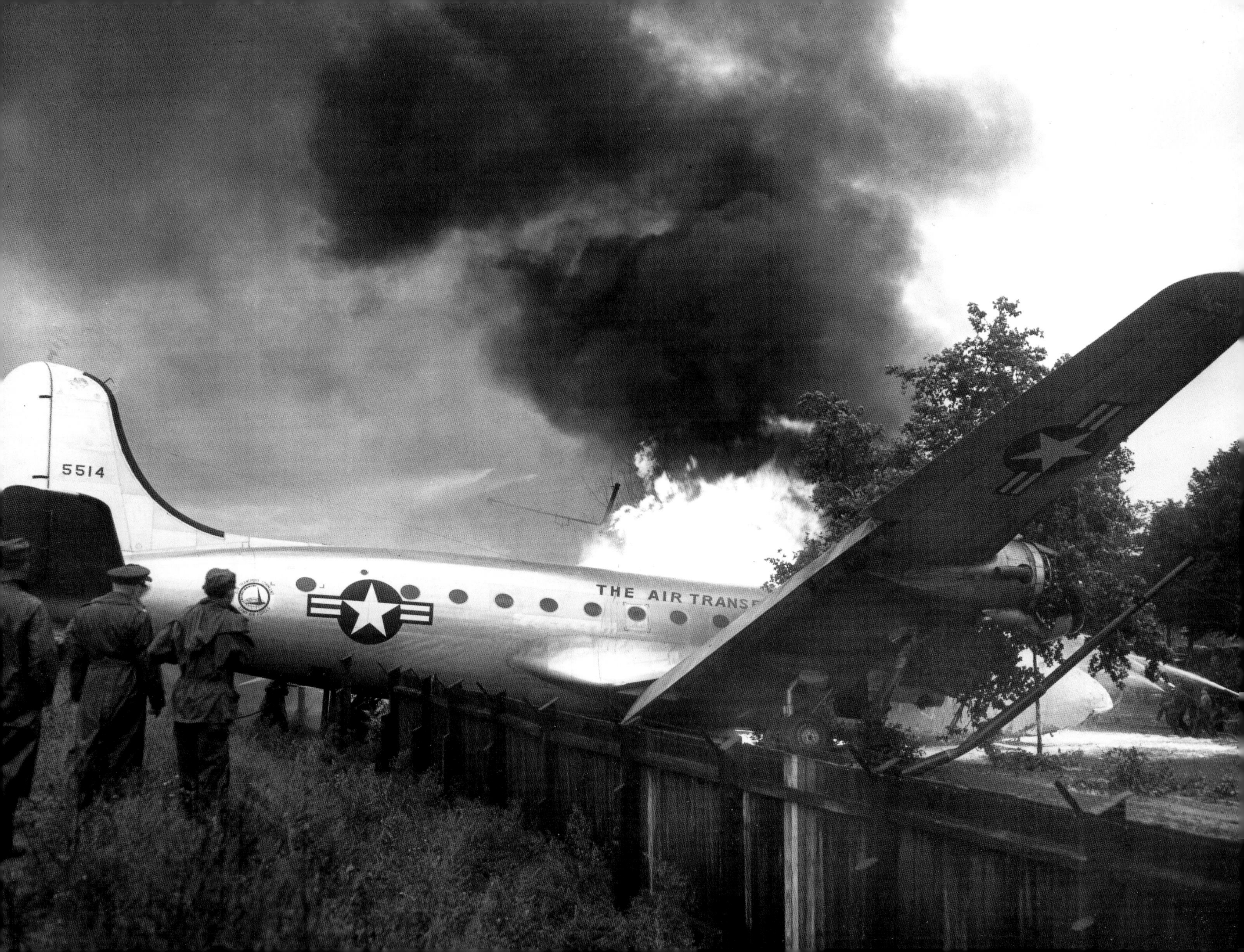
5514
THE AIR TRANS

9. THE AIRLIFT CRASHES

On August 13, 1948, a Friday, while General Tunner was on a flight going into Tempelhof, three C-54s ahead of his aircraft crash-landed on final approach in weather approaching zero-zero visibility and below IFR (instrument) minimums. On top of

► Two US pilots were injured, one seriously, and two others escaped injury when this Navy C-54 on an Airlift flight to West Berlin crashed at Tempelhof Airfield November 16, 1948. It was carrying 10 tons of coal and overshot the runway while landing in a heavy fog. NARA

►► A rain-soaked MP stands guard over the charred wreckage of a C-54 which overshot the runway at Tempelhof Air Field in West Berlin on August 13,1948 and burst into flames, after crashing through a fence on the edge of the field. The plane was flying coal on an Airlift flight to West Berlin. NARA

this, there was a cloudburst that temporarily obscured the radar operators' screens as they were guiding the aircraft on final. "With all that confusion on the ground, the traffic control people began stacking up the planes coming in… (soon) the stack was packed from three thousand to twelve thousand feet."[1]

Three C-54s crash landed and it quickly became obvious that Tunner had to make some radical changes. Tunner immediately ordered that all flights fly under instrument flight rules and ordered that if they couldn't land on the first approach, they would immediately return to West Germany. This enabled 3 minute spacing for aircraft going

▲ This C-47 was a casualty of the Berlin Airlift. Date and location unknown.

into Tempelhof. Tunner also realized that he would have to find 225 C-54s, supplemented by C-47s and British aircraft, to get the bare minimum of 4,500 tons per day to support the civilian and military population in West Berlin.

"On April 5, 1949, a scheduled BEA passenger Vickers Viking was coming in to land at Gatow when a Soviet Yak

▲ On July 25, 1948, a U. S. Air Force C-47 crashed into a house in West Berlin (the Steglitz Friedenau District). The pilot, Charles H. King, and co-pilot were killed. No one in the nearby housing was killed or badly injured. A street in West Berlin was then named after Charles H. King.

fighter, which had been observed for some time performing aerobatics in the area, suddenly dived, passed underneath it, then rose sharply and ripped off the Viking's starboard wing. Both planes crashed. The Russian pilot, the British crew and seven passengers were killed."[2] Both sides cried foul but it was obvious that the Yak fighter was flying recklessly. The Viking was on a scheduled flight and the Russians were not properly monitoring its path or its communications.

Bad weather accounted for the majority of the crashes but the survival rate was good, considering the number of Airlift flights. "In all, 31 Americans, 41 British (including an Australian and a South African), and 5 German civilians lost their lives in airlift operations."[3]

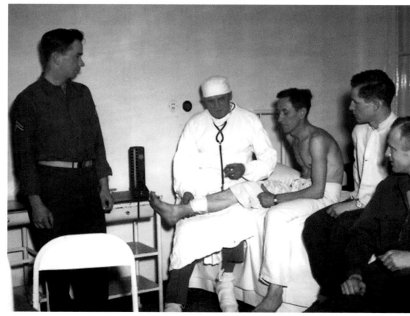

▲ On Monday April 5, 1948, a British European Airways Vickers Viking airliner crashed near RAF Gatow, after a mid-air collision with a Soviet Yak-3 fighter. All ten passengers and four crew on board the Viking were killed, as well as the Soviet pilot. In this photo, a Russian officer is examining the wreckage. The incident heightened tensions between the Allies and the Russians.
© AlliiertenMuseum / Berlin

In March 1949, during the Berlin Airlift, survivors of a crash in the Soviet Zone consult with a doctor before they return to West Berlin.
Author's Collection

▶ The funeral of a Royal Air Force aircrew at the British cemetery in West Berlin, July 19, 1949. Five RAF crewmen were killed when their Handley Page Hastings crashed on takeoff from Tegel airport in West Berlin on July 15th. IMPERIAL WAR MUSEUM

THE MYSTERIOUS YAK-28 CRASH

Story & Photos Courtesy of Leo Chrzanowski & Gene Kyle

Some 17 years after the Airlift, on April 6, 1966, a top secret Soviet two-seat bomber, a Yakovlev Yak-28, crashed into the Havelsee, a lake straddling the British and Russian sectors of Berlin.

The British immediately mounted a salvage operation, promising to return the aircraft and the bodies of its two pilots to the Russians.

But as a barge and a crane were set up on the lake's surface to recover the aircraft, beneath the surface, a very different operation was in progress–taking its top-secret technology back to Britain where it could be examined.

The first the British knew of the Havelsee incident was when radio operators at Berlin's RAF Gatow Airfield picked up a message from the aircraft's controllers ordering the pilot to try to land in the lake, but inside the Soviet sector.

Despite a valiant attempt, he failed, his aircraft falling short and inside the British zone. Brigadier David Wilson, a spy operative in Berlin, was playing squash when the aircraft came down. A quarter of an hour later, still in his shorts, he coordinated one of the most astonishing espionage coups of the Cold War.

British military police cordoned off the scene and an interpreter was sent to the lakeside, where Russian troops commanded by General Vladimir Bulanov were trying to force their way through. They watched in frustration as Squadron Leader Maurice Taylor rowed to the wreckage to take photographs.

The top-secret fighter was later identified as a Yak-28, NATO codename Firebar. It had a unique radar capability. Britain and the United States were desperate to know what made it so effective. Now they had their chance. It was 10:09 pm on day one, nearly seven hours after the crash. Interpreters were ordered to do everything they could to buy time, trying to mollify the concerned Bulanov.

At the same time, technical experts examined the aircraft's Skipspin radar, which, unlike the current western systems, could look up and down as well as straight ahead.

Down below the water, one British serviceman was trying to get the pilots' bodies out of the aircraft so they could concentrate on examining the radar unit.

By 1:45pm on the second day, the bodies had been bagged up and, below the water, work was going on to remove the radar. Meanwhile, Major Geoffrey Stephenson, one of the British interpreters, persuaded Bulanov that they were still trying to recover the bodies of the crew.

At 4:07 the next morning, the bodies were slipped onto a raft. As dawn broke, the Russians were informed they had been recovered and would be handed over that evening. What the Russians did not see was the divers attaching the jet engines by line to the launch which then dragged them along behind it under

water, and took them to a jetty a mile from the wreck, where they were loaded into crates and flown back to Farnborough for examination. Meanwhile, the pilots' bodies were handed over to Bulanov. Within 48 hours, the engines and the cockpit radar unit had been carefully returned to the Firebar's wreckage. On April 13, the barge was moved to the Soviet sector where the wreckage was turned over to the Russians. As the engines were handed over, Bulanov looked at them and could clearly see that the tips of some of the rotor blades had been sawn off. "He didn't say a word," Stephenson said. "He simply looked at me and shrugged, as if to say: 'I've been screwed', and of course he had."

Then, the Russians discovered that something was missing. The British insisted that everything had been handed over. If anything was missing it must still be down on the floor of the Havelsee.

What was missing? The Russians were unable to reply. They could hardly acknowledge that it was a top-secret radar dish. They just had to hope that it was on the bottom of the lake. The resultant changes to RAF aircraft, to deceive the Skipspin radar, restored parity in the Cold War.

ENDNOTES
1   D. M. Giangreco and Robert Griffin, Airbridge to Berlin, p. 122-123
2   A. & J. Tusa, The Berlin Airlift, p. 116
3   Ibid. p.109

▲ Story and all Photos courtesy of Leo Chrzanowski / Gene Kyle

LAST VITTLES FLIGHT
17835727 TONS AIRLIFTED
TO BERLIN

UNITED STATES AIR FOR

10. AFTERMATH

On May 12, 1949, after an agreement with the United Nations, the four powers agreed to end the Berlin blockade. The following message was broadcast: "Agreement has now been reached between the three Western powers and the Soviets regarding raising the Berlin Blockade and the holding of a meeting

◄ The last Airlift flight to West Berlin left Rhein-Main Air Base on September 30, 1949.
USAF National Museum

► Navy VR-6 Squadron personnel celebrate the end of the Berlin Blockade on May 12, 1949 at Rhein-Main Air Force Base.
German Federal Press Office

and fresh fish reached Berlin…seven coal trains and five passenger trains arrived…Berliners were not exultant; they were suspicious and afraid."[2]

A New York Times reporter, Sydney Gruson "asked the first German he met, a policeman, what he thought and the man answered: 'What can we be expected to think after living for ten months under blockade? We want life to be a little easier. We want more light, we want more gas, and perhaps more than anything, an end to dehydrated potatoes.'"[3]

Like the West Berliners, the Allies realized that there could be more blockades, so they kept some airlift resources in place in West Germany in case there were further conflicts with the Russians, who systematically made excuses to slow down rail and road access to Berlin.

Even after the East Germans built the Wall on August 13, 1961 to prevent people from escaping from East Berlin, there were standoffs between U. S. and Russian military units well into the 1960s. So military units stayed in place in both the Allied sectors in Berlin and the Russian sector. The Wall did not prevent some 30,000 refugees fleeing East Germany every month.

"There were indeed covert operations underway, as there had been since victory in 1945. Western intelligence used Berlin as a listening post. It could gather information about what was going on in Eastern Europe…One major intelligence-gathering effort was the Berlin Tunnel Operation. A tunnel was constructed by the CIA, snaking out into the eastern sector of the city, allowing them to

of the Council of Foreign Ministers. All communications, transportation and trade restrictions imposed by both sides…and between Berlin and the Eastern Zones will be removed May 12…" [1]

The Allied airlift pilots jumped for joy, realizing that they soon would rotate back to the States or England. But the cautious West Berliners did not dance in the streets. "The first lorries (trucks) came into the city draped in banners and garlands and were met by small groups, curious rather than jubilant…A few marvels signaled that the blockade had ended. Within hours of the opening of the barriers at Marienborn oranges and lemons, cucumbers

◄ On September 30, 1949, this C-54 landed at Tempelhof Airfield, marking the end of the Berlin Airlift. The flight crew celebrated by displaying a sign "For Sale…Slightly Used Airline…" The C-54 carried the last load of 'air-hauled' coal, and a group of correspondents. NARA

monitor (sensitive military) telephone calls…it caused immense embarrassment to the KGB."[4]

West Berlin continued its fast track re-construction while East Berlin remained a city of empty, desolate buildings. The only significant new buildings there were Stalinist government buildings and monuments. Ultimately, the Berlin Wall came down in 1989, and Germany was finally on its way to re-unification. Allied military units stationed in Berlin were just memories. But the Berlin Airlift has gone down in history as the biggest and most successful airlift of all time.

ENDNOTES

1 Arthur Pearcy, *Berlin Airlift*, p. 111
2 A. & J. Tusa, *The Berlin Airlift*, p. 357
3 Richard Reeves, *Daring Young Men*, p. 261
4 J. Sutherland & D. Cantwell, *Berlin Airlift*, p.172

◀ On May 11, 1949 at Helmstedt, two trains loaded with coal and other vital supplies await the end of the blockade before departing for West Berlin.
NARA

▶ In 1949, a West German boy, shielding his eyes from sun, stares down empty tracks at Charlottenburg station awaiting the first train after the Berlin blockade ended.
NARA

◄ After the blockade, this was the first train into West Berlin, pulled by a Russian locomotive. It carried journalists and passengers from Helmstedt. NARA

► In July 1949, this U.S. Army convoy brought in food for Army units in West Berlin. Military police escorted the convoy as it passed through the Soviet zone. NARA

◄ Berliners celebrate the restoration of road links between West Berlin and Hanover after the lifting of the blockade, May 12, 1949. The sign on the front of the first bus reads 'Hurra Wir Leben Noch' (Hurray! We are still Alive!).
IMPERIAL WAR MUSEUM

► In May 1949, crowds filled Rathaus, Schöneberg, to celebrate the end of the Berlin Blockade. The Allies, though, continued a limited Airlift to keep West Berlin well stocked with coal, food, and other critical supplies.
LANDESARCHIV BERLIN

◀ In 1949, West Berlin's Mayor Ernst Reuter dedicates "Platz der Luftbrücke" (Airlift Square), marking the first anniversary of the Airlift.

▲ West Berlin's Mayor, Ernst Reuter, commenting to huge crowds at the end of the blockade declared, "We called on the world for help. The world heard our cry."

◄ The dedication of the Berlin Airlift Memorial in Luftbrücke Platz in 1952.
USAF

▲ Willi Brandt returned to Germany after World War II. In 1948, he started his political career, holding various offices within the Social Democratic Party (SPD) and becoming a member of the German parliament. Brandt first became well known outside Germany when he took the position of mayor of West Berlin, which he held from 1957 until 1966. This was a particularly tense time for the city, with the building of the Berlin Wall in 1961.
GERMAN ARCHIVES

▲ General Lucius Clay and Willi Brandt review Berlin police in 1962.
AUTHOR'S COLLECTION

◄ One of many signs that delineated the various sectors of Berlin.
AUTHOR'S COLLECTION

► Downtown West Berlin in 1956. Heavy traffic on the Kudamm was not unusual. East Berlin, by contrast, was desolate and most of the buildings had not been replaced or rebuilt.
AUTHOR'S COLLECTION

◀◀ (Previous spread) Russian soldiers march by the Soviet War Memorial, celebrating the founding of the Red Army. Date unknown. Author's Collection

◀ In the 1950s, Scottish infantry, accompanied by an umpire and three young West Berliners, march to the Grunewald forest for an exercise. Author's Collection

▶ In 1952, U.S. Army M-47 medium tanks participate in a military parade in West Berlin. Author's Collection

▶ French GIAT AMX-13 tanks ready for inspection in West Berlin, 1959. © Bruce McAllister

MONDOVI

▲ In 1959, the French 46th Infantry en route to training exercise in the French Sector of West Berlin.
© Bruce McAllister

▶ In 1972, new barriers went up in Bernauer Strasse, West Berlin. They were immediately labeled the "Modern Frontier." The East Germans reinforced the border with broken bottles set in concrete, and tank traps.
Author's Collection

▲ Tensions came to a head on October 27, 1961, when U. S. Army tanks and armored vehicles took up positions at Checkpoint Charlie and faced down Soviet armored vehicles. Eventually, both sides backed down and the tank standoff ended with no shots fired.
AUTHOR'S COLLECTION

► A VOPO (East German Border Guard) looks into West Berlin. Date unknown.

◀ Under the shadow of the Brandenburg Gate, a sign warns West Berliners that East Berlin is beyond the barbed wire. A water cannon reinforces the warning. Researchers estimate that From August 1961 until November 1989 over 125 Berliners were killed, trying to escape East Berlin. Before the construction of the Berlin Wall in 1961, 3.5 million East Germans circumvented Eastern Bloc emigration restrictions, many by escaping from East Berlin into West Berlin, from where they could then make their way to West Germany.

BUNDESARCHIV

▶ In 1959, Russian soldiers served as the honor guard at the Soviet War Memorial in East Berlin. The monument was built in 1945 and commemorated the 80,000 Russian soldiers who perished during the Battle of Berlin.

© BRUCE MCALLISTER

◄ Russian
military personnel
take a break in
East Berlin in
1959.
© Bruce McAllister

► In 1959, East
Berlin did not
have much traffic.
© Bruce McAllister

◄ In March 1962, VOPOs discovered this tunnel from East Berlin to West Berlin. An unknown number of Berliners had used it before its discovery.
AUTHOR'S COLLECTION

► In 1956, the Russians discovered a tunnel from West Berlin to East Berlin that the CIA had built to monitor Russian military communications. The 450-meter-long tunnel, built in 1955, led from Rudow in West Berlin to Alt-Glienicke in Soviet-occupied East Berlin. By tapping into the enemy's underground cables, Allied intelligence agents recorded 440,000 phone calls, gaining a clearer picture of Red Army maneuvers in eastern Germany. It was a big embarassment for the Russians.
AUTHOR'S COLLECTION

▲ At the Checkpoint Charlie Museum, a visitor studies the cart that was used in 1964 to help 57 East Berliners escape through an elaborate tunnel.
AUTHOR'S COLLECTION

◀ F-84Fs of the USAF Air National Guard in Newfoundland, November 1961, prior to flying the Atlantic to Europe in response to the Berlin Crisis. Because of the long over-water distance to the next airfield in the Azores, the planes were towed to the end of the runway prior to takeoff to conserve fuel. During this Operation Stair Step deployment of more than 200 fighter aircraft (the largest overseas movement of a fighter force since World War II), not a single plane was lost.
USAF

▶ In 1952, East German workers clear a killing zone near the Helmstedt checkpoint on the British-Russian border. The East German authorities claimed too many people were infiltrating their zone.
AUTHOR'S COLLECTION

▲ In 1949, as the Berlin Airlift ended, the Soviet authorities removed many railroad tracks and ties around East Berlin.

BIBLIOGRAPHY

Aviation Operations, *A Special Study of Operation Vittles*, New York, NY, 1949

Bering, Henrik, *Outpost Berlin*, edition Q, Carol Stream, IL, 1995

Clay, Lucius D., *Decision in Germany*, Doubleday & Co., New York, NY, 1950

Collier, Richard, *Bridge Across The Sky*, McGraw-Hill, New York, NY, 1978

Donovan, Frank, *Bridge in the Sky*. David McKay, New York, NY, 1968

Giangreco D.M. & Griffin, R., *Air Bridge to Berlin,* Presidio Press, Novato, CA, 1988

Grathwol, Robert, & Moorhus, Donita, *Berlin & the American Military*
New York University Press, New York, NY, 1999

Howley, Frank, *Berlin Command,* Putnam, New York, NY, 1950

Jackson, Robert, *The Berlin Airlift,* Patrick Stephens, Wellingborough, UK, 1988

McCullough, David, *Truman*, Simon & Schuster Paperbacks, New York, NY, 1992

Miller, Roger, *To Save a City – The Berlin Airlift, 1948-1949*
Texas A&M Military History Series, TX, 2008

Nelson, Daniel J., *Wartime Origins of the Berlin Dilemma.*
University of Alabama Press, AL, 1978

Parrish, Thomas, *Berlin in The Balance- 1945-1949*
Addison Wesley, Reading, MA, 1998

Pearcy, Arthur, *Berlin Airlift*, Airlife Publishing, Shrewsbury, England, 1997

Provan, John & Davis, R.E.G., Berlin *Airlift: The Effort & the Airplanes*
Paladwr Publishers, McLean, VA, 1998

Reeves, Richard, *Daring Young Men*, Simon & Schuster, New York, NY, 2010

Smith, Jean Edward, *The Defense of Berlin*
The Johns Hopkins Press, Baltimore, MD, 1963

Ibid, *Lucius D. Clay*, Henry Holt & Company, New York, NY, 1990

Tusa, Ann and John, *The Berlin Airlift*, Atheneum, New York, NY 1988

◀ (Overleaf) Some forty years after the Airlift, President Reagan made an emotional speech at the Brandenburg Gate when he declared "Mr. Gorbachev, tear down this wall!" That's exactly what happened as young Berliners took sledgehammers to the Wall.
AUTHOR'S COLLECTION